The Lead Carpenter Handbook

The Complete, Hands-On Guide to Successful Job-Site Management

◆ ◆ ◆ ◆ ◆

by Timothy Faller

Foreword by Linda Case

A Journal of Light Construction Book

Editorial Director: Steven Bliss
Editor: Kathy Price-Robinson
Production Editor: Josie Masterson-Glen
Production Manager: Theresa Emerson
Book Designer: Annie Clark
Photographs by Bill Robinson

International Standard Book Number: 0-9632268-7-8
Library of Congress Catalog Card Number: 98-074276
Printed in the United States of America

A Journal of Light Construction Book
The Journal of Light Construction is a tradename of Hanley-Wood, LLC.

The Journal of Light Construction
186 Allen Brook Lane
Williston, VT 05495

About The Author

Timothy Faller is a veteran contractor and production manager, and former lead carpenter. Based on his extensive field experience throughout the building and remodeling business, Tim has developed and conducted many lead carpenter training programs across the country, and helped develop the NARI Certified Lead Carpenter program.

Training & Consulting

Tim also offers education, training, and consulting services to building and remodeling firms nationwide. For more information, contact Field Training Services via email at tfaller206@worldnet.att.net or visit on the web at www.leadcarpenter.com.

Lead Carpenter Audiobook

Based on Tim's popular training workshops, this complete set of four 90-minute tapes provides a comprehensive approach to planning and implementing the Lead Carpenter system. To order, visit www.leadcarpenter.com.

Acknowledgements

Just like we need people to help us through life in general, the successful completion of this book is the combined effort of many people. Special thank you is due to many for helping with this book.

Thank you to my bosses and friends, Mike Denker and Guy Semmes, for their support and encouragement in developing training for lead carpenters and also for encouraging me to write this book. Guy originally signed me up, without my knowledge, to work on a pilot training course for lead carpenters — which eventually became the basis for the Certified Lead Carpenters program from NARI. Mike has continually supported my participation in seminars and conferences, which have given me education and materials to draw upon, even though it often meant he had to carry my load on the job for a few days.

Thank you to the team of people that provided all the technical help needed by any amateur writer: to Kathy Price-Robinson for editing and positive reinforcement, to Josie Masterson-Glen for scheduling, encouraging timeliness, and actually producing the book. Thank you to all The Journal of Light Construction staff, past and present, who gave me encouragement to keep this idea alive and bring it to reality.

No acknowledgment would be complete without expressing appreciation to the home front for persevering with me. A special thanks to my wife, who always encouraged the writing of this book, even through the roller coaster ride of trying to find someone to publish it. A special thanks to my kids, who think it's cool that Dad wrote a book, and for being patient and letting Dad get this done.

Timothy Faller

Foreword

By Linda Case

The most difficult challenge in a growing company is the development of "systems." A system is a known and tested way to accomplish a task or series of tasks that allows for a predictable outcome for the customer.

McDonald's made their money not with hamburgers and shakes — those were available everywhere and often in a tastier form. McDonald's made their fortune by developing a system that made it easy for their franchisees and employees to deliver their products and services predictably. Think of the most successful businesses — whether it's Price Club, Home Depot, Federal Express, UPS, or Jiffy-Lube — and behind each one's success you'll find strong systems that support fairly ordinary employees. Those systems are the reason that repeat customers can anticipate a positive buying experience and a satisfactory level of product quality and service before they walk in the door.

Those of us in smaller businesses must strive mightily to create the systems that will support our employees in delivering our vision to the market place. In a tiny business, the systems often exist only in the head of the owner. But as the business grows, the contents of the owner's brain must be distilled into a set of procedures that can be written down and taught to employees.

Tim Faller's book is about establishing a Lead Carpenter System in your company. Why? Because what area of your business is more unruly, more unpredictable, more subject to turnover than production? When your company was small, you made sure the quality was there personally. To do so you wore many hats. You sold the job, you estimated the job, you wrote up the contract, and then you put your belt on and did the job.

As your company grows, responsibility for different parts of that continuum, from sales to production, are assumed by different employees. But quality often suffers. In the past, construction companies tried to overcome this decrease in quality by paying supervisors to find the mistakes and then paying field staff to rework them. Tim Faller rightly points out, however, that depending on rework is expensive in time, money, and client satisfaction. Rather, empower the smart field employees you've hired. Only by pushing decision-making and management to the field level can you overcome the expense of supervising quality into the job. You want quality built into the job — built right the first time. That can only come from a responsible, well-trained, accountable field work force.

In my thirty years of remodeling experience — the first half from within a remodeling company, the second half working with hundreds of contractors of all sizes and types — I have seen one company after another try to invent the Lead Carpenter System, whether they knew it or not. How do you estimate for waste and mismanagement, for inaccurate or missing communication, for lack of training and technical knowledge? You don't. Your profitability and competitiveness is based on doing it right at the front line level of production. Now, how do you do that?

A well-planned and thoughtfully implemented Lead Carpenter System is the answer. Contractors have been crying out for a book that tells them how to achieve this. I can't imagine a book more chock full of ideas and solutions — not just from Tim's company, but from many other contractors as well. I particularly applaud Tim's non-dogmatic and open-minded approach which says, "Take from this idea buffet whatever will help you in your company." Tim doesn't present one job description, but many. He leaves open to choice whether your company will need a production manager, and, most importantly, he clearly recognizes the difference between the ideal and the real.

Distilled into this well-written book are thousands of hours of research and learning. You are lucky to have found such a resource!

Linda Case is president of Remodelers Advantage, Inc. in Silver Spring, Maryland.

Contents

Introduction   A Strategy for Growth 3

Chapter 1   A New Management System 11

Chapter 2   Pros, Cons, and Objections Answered . . .29

Chapter 3   Progressive Implementation 41

Chapter 4   Developing a Job Description 51

Chapter 5   Hiring and Training 61

Chapter 6   The Production Manager's Role 73

Chapter 7   Profit and the Lead Carpenter 81

Chapter 8   Good Job Planning 91

Chapter 9   Site Supervision 119

Chapter 10   Post-Job Responsibilities 139

Chapter 11   Frequently Asked Questions 143

Chapter 12   Four Case Studies 153

APPENDICES

Appendix A   Forms for Job-Site Management 165

Appendix B   Lead Carpenter Survey 181

Appendix C   Lead Carpenter Training Segments 185

Index 203

Introduction: A Strategy for Growth

WITH HARD WORK AND A LITTLE LUCK, A TIME COMES FOR EVERY REMODELING OR custom building company when there is more work than the contractor can do, more jobs than the contractor can supervise, and more tasks than a single person can handle in any given day. With the harried contractor rushing from job to job during the day (scheduling, ordering, and putting out fires) and cranking out bids and estimates during the evenings and weekends, every element of the company begins to suffer. The contractor's family and personal life often suffer as well.

Eventually, it's time to spread out the duties and responsibilities among more people. This is where the lead carpenter system comes in, which means a carpenter on the job is given the power to "own" the job: to plan it, schedule and supervise subs, supervise other employees, and deal effectively with the client, as well as perform carpentry.

I know how this system can transform a company because I have been both a lead carpenter and a production manager supervising other lead carpenters, and before that, I owned my own contracting company. My belief is that a lead carpenter system, when implemented correctly, can allow a remodeling enterprise to grow and prosper while maintaining the attention to detail typically found in a one-person company. The goal of this book, therefore, is to provide a blueprint for a lead carpenter system, which you can implement in your small- to mid-sized construction company.

While I'll refer throughout this book primarily to remodeling companies, many of the issues discussed apply as well to small custom building

Note: In the interests of clear and simple writing, the pronouns "he" and "his" are used in this book to refer to lead carpenters and contractors. But it is important to point out that an increasing number of women are working successfully in the building trades as carpenters, managers, and owners.

companies and to companies that do both remodeling and custom building. So while the lead carpenter system has been developed primarily to help remodelers, it can be adapted readily to custom builders. And for the sake of clarity, I will use the term "contractor" to refer throughout the book to the company owner, whether that person is a remodeling contractor or custom home builder.

I'd also like to note here that this book outlines the lead carpenter system and its implementation in somewhat idealized situations as envisioned by the author and experts in the field. But very few companies fit into any mold perfectly, and no two are identical, so modifications will have to be made to the systems and procedures described here. I recommend that you read through the book, pick out what you can use and apply it to your company where you wish. Then, reread the book later for continued ideas and growth.

WHY THE SYSTEM DEVELOPED

It's easy to see how the lead carpenter system developed when you analyze the different types of construction projects and their specific management needs. For instance, the position of site superintendent has evolved in the area of new home development because of the need to supervise a number of home projects being built at the same time on contiguous sites. Likewise, large commercial developments function best with a project manager on hand who may not be a tradesman but who has the organizational skills needed to keep a large project running smoothly (see "Definition of Terms" below).

In the remodeling industry, the lead carpenter system developed to meet the specific demands found on jobs that are too small for a full-time supervisor to be cost-effective, but where there are so many job-site issues that supervision from a distance can lead to costly mistakes. Therefore, it makes perfect sense to give the responsibility for the supervision of a job site to a person—in this case, a carpenter—who is already working there.

PROBLEMS UNIQUE TO REMODELING

In remodeling, several conditions exist that require the degree of supervision that a lead carpenter can offer. First, there are the difficulties of dealing with an existing building. The floors are out of level. Termites may have taken up residence. The walls are $5^1/2$ inches thick instead of $4^9/16$ inches. If you've done much remodeling, I'm sure you can relate all too well. On these jobs, someone has to sort out how the new structure will tie into the existing and how the new and old finishes will blend. How will the new floor match the level of the existing? This is the kind of decision-making that begins at the start of the job and lasts throughout

NEW HOUSE/OLD HOUSE: Job-Site Dynamics

New Construction	Remodeling
Sometimes working with a homeowner	Always working with a homeowner
New materials and site	Working with existing conditions
Dirt and dust don't matter	Cleanliness matters
Client does not yet have emotional attachment to the home	Client is emotionally attached to the home
May not be neighbors to worry about	Always neighbors to worry about
No details to match	Many details to match
Very predictable schedule pattern	Unpredictable schedule pattern
Never pets or children living on site	Often pets and children on site
Sometimes many homes in one location	Usually locations are miles apart

The job-site dynamics for new homes and remodeling projects are very different. The lead carpenter supervising a remodel often faces more complicated issues on the site.

the project. These decisions cannot be made in haste or at a drafting table. They must be made by someone intimately involved with the job.

The second problem particular to remodeling projects is the presence of a homeowner. Of course, owners are involved in other building situations, such as new custom homes, but on those jobs you do not have owners living on the construction site. The presence of owners creates a number of problems. For example, homeowners often want to discuss the job first thing in the morning. They have questions about how the project looks or the location of a window. They are concerned about lead in the air and the dust on the floor. They invariably have a cat or dog that needs to be looked after during the day. They need the house secured against theft and weather at the end of the day. They worry about allowing subcontractors into their home (their sanctuary) and whether or not these subs are doing a good job. Plus, living on a construction site makes homeowners more than a little cranky. Often, they need some "hand-holding" and calming down. These are issues that cannot be effectively addressed from the office or supervised from the truck—even with a cell phone.

The third problem is the need to carefully supervise subcontractors. This is not because they can't do their work, but because of the complications in working in an older home. Reworking an old structure to meet current codes and standards often involves creative on-the-job problem solving. And even the best designers can't see through walls and know what you will run into. Surprises are the norm.

Add to that the continuous changes to the schedule, the need to complete some work out of sequence, and the need for decisions to be made quickly. Often the project is small enough, for example, that the plumber has allotted only half a day for his work. If a decision that affects the plumbing cannot be made quickly, the plumber may walk away and not be able to return for several days.

Having a lead carpenter on the site to address these kinds of problems can bring peace of mind to the client as well as the contractor. Indeed, peace of mind, greater profits, and the potential for growth—while preserving your sanity—are what the lead carpenter system is all about.

DEFINITION OF TERMS

Because different terms are used in different parts of the country, and from one company to the next, this is a good time to define how key terms will be used throughout the book. For instance, while the lead carpenter position we are discussing is sometimes referred to as the "project manager," I use the latter term in a different sense.

Here are the definitions for the key terms used in this book:

• *Project Manager:* This term applies to an individual who assumes management of an entire project. This is a person not working with his tools (and, in fact, may not even be a tradesperson) but whose main responsibility is to manage the flow of work, coordinate trades, and bring the project to completion. This is a term more typically used in commercial work, but is also used in large-scale residential construction.

• *Site Superintendent:* This refers to individuals who supervise an entire site, usually containing more than one home, such as a new home development. "Supes" are there on the site to supervise and coordinate. They spend a large amount of time scheduling so that the subs are working to maximum efficiency.

• *Production Manager:* This is the term for individuals who are typically based off-site and travel from job site to job site. They have responsibility for more than one job in different locales, and give on-site direction—often specific instruction on the work to be accomplished that day. They also order material, schedule subs, etc. This role is often played by the owner of a remodeling company (if they don't have carpenters on the jobs that they can trust) until the jobs become too numerous to handle.

• *Lead Carpenter:* I use this term to refer to a tradesperson who assumes management responsibility while continuing to work with his hands on the job. These jobs are typically smaller in nature than the jobs a project manager would manage—anywhere from $10,000 to as high as $500,000. For larger jobs, it is probably cost-effective to use a project manager.

WHO NEEDS A LEAD CARPENTER SYSTEM?

The lead carpenter system described in this book works best on full-scale remodeling projects. These are projects that involve an addition or substantial renovation work where the remodeling company will be in the home for a month or more, and the remodeler wants to use his own employees to perform the carpentry work. These projects typically involve several trades and a variety of materials.

The size of a company and the number of jobs produced each year will also dictate the use of this system. Obviously, if a company has one job going at a time, and the owner chooses to work on that job, a lead carpenter would not be necessary.

Let's look now at the typical evolution of remodeling companies. Most often they start out with a person who has some experience in the trades and who wants to "go it on his own." He has the truck, a couple of jobs lined up, and has just taken the test for a contractor's license. In the beginning, these brave and hardworking people don all the hats — manager, salesman, bookkeeper, carpenter, and helper. As the work proceeds, most realize this is not as much fun or as profitable as they had thought, and some return to the relatively simple life of working for someone else.

However, a fair number like the challenge of being the boss and recognize the need to have assistance. Usually, the first employee is a helper, someone to dig, clean, cut, nail, etc. As the business grows, the company owner recognizes the need to be gone from the job regularly during the day to make sales calls, prepare bills, perhaps collect a check. This creates a need to hire a carpenter who can "run" the job while he is gone.

The need for a lead occurs when one or more of the following conditions exist:

Greater Sales Volume

When the company reaches a sales volume that can no longer be produced by one person, the owner then needs help meeting all the demands of scheduling, ordering, communicating, and supervising. This volume level will vary for every person and every company, and will also depend on the number of jobs it takes to reach that volume. For instance, if a company is doing $500,000 of work in a year, but it's done on only one or two jobs, the owner will want to stay involved. It would be counter-productive, and therefore not profitable, for the owner to hand only one or two jobs over to a lead carpenter. But if the same company is doing $500,000 a year with eight jobs, the owner will want some help with the production and supervision of each job.

Anticipated Growth in Sales

Sales leads have increased and there is a happy expectation that the company will grow. Of course, we must recognize that not all people want their companies to grow. We have seen and read about people who never want to move away from the field; they enjoy the construction part of the business, and the company is profitable. If that is their goal, they should keep it that way. But if the expectation is that the company will grow, and the leads are increasing, the owner will need to delegate some part of the business to someone else. This someone else can be either a new salesman or a lead carpenter. In the first case, the owner can remain in the field and stay involved in hands-on production, and in the second case, the owner can continue to do sales and marketing and delegate the production work to the lead carpenter, or several lead carpenters on several jobs.

Desire for Time Off

We change, as we age and mature, and our lives must change. Marriage, children, and aging bodies all contribute to the need to share the responsibility or load of a construction company with others. Many people work 60 to 80 hours a week to keep the business running, or perhaps just afloat. For some, this is what keeps us young; for others, it brings gray hair. These people need some relief. A vacation. A long weekend. As you may know, families demand more and more time as the kids get into Little League, Scouts, soccer, and other social activities. In short, delegation to the lead carpenter allows a contractor time to enjoy life outside the company.

WHO DOESN'T NEED A LEAD CARPENTER SYSTEM?

One question I am often asked in my lead carpenter seminars is: Will this system work with new home construction? The answer depends on several factors. One is the size of the house. Just like the size of a remodel, the size of the project will determine whether the lead carpenter is really a lead carpenter or a project manager. The difference lies in how much he uses any tools other than a calculator or tape measure. Many new home projects are large enough to warrant a full-time superintendent rather than a lead carpenter. If the project is small enough that a carpenter can work on the site and manage the job, the system will work.

The second factor that might preclude the lead carpenter system in new home building is the source of labor. If a company is building a house primarily with its own labor (that is, the company has the carpenters on the payroll), then this system will work. However, if the company decides to subcontract out all the labor and simply be the general contractor, the system does not fit, mainly because there won't be a carpenter employed by the company on the job from start to finish. Because the labor on the job would be subcontractors that come and go, the benefit of continuity is lost and must be supplied by a site superintendent or a project manager. This person fills management roles but does not provide the carpentry labor.

Another reason a lead carpenter system is not as critical in new home building is that a new home does not require the same constant supervision as a remodel. Therefore, it is difficult to justify the added cost of having a person in a management position who could be spending more time "producing." Indeed, the lead carpenter system does cost more to run, but in remodeling the expense makes sense, while in new home building it may not make sense.

Also, for smaller remodeling projects like siding replacement, window replacement, or other jobs that take only one to ten days to complete, you are better off with a modified lead carpenter system. For example, if the project is to replace kitchen cabinets and a countertop, the preliminary work—measuring, ordering, and scheduling—will fall into the hands of someone who sees the job eight weeks before the lead carpenter begins work. However, once the job starts, the lead carpenter will still be responsible for quality control, talking to the homeowner, keeping the site clean, and other job-site functions.

In Chapter One, I'll explain exactly how the system works, how the team members involved with a project interact with each other, and the best communication methods to make the lead carpenter system "sing." ◢

Chapter 1

A New Management System

L*ET'S ASSUME THAT WHAT YOU'VE READ AND HEARD ABOUT THE LEAD CARPENTER* system has piqued your interest. What does this creature look like? How would it change your existing company? If I put it on paper, what would the organizational chart look like? More importantly, how would it operate?

Every company has an operating system. Some are written down, some are simply in the contractor's head, and some have developed over years and fall into the category of "that's just the way we do it." Changing this can be difficult, so the goal must be clear. This chapter will give you a comparative look at operating systems, including the standard system you may be using now, and the new system this book is illustrating.

In a small company, the typical supervision system of management involves the contractor spending a fair amount of time on the road inspecting and managing the work on several jobs. He is responsible for every aspect of the job, from assigning tasks to the carpenters and laborers to scheduling subs, ordering materials, and meeting with clients. This works well with one or two jobs. The contractor has immediate contact with the job and, consequently, significant control.

However, this system can become a liability if you plan to grow your business. Growth will require that some of the authority and responsibility be carried by someone else. One way to achieve growth is to add a supervisor, typically called a production manager, who essentially duplicates the contractor's role but leaves him time to sell or run the business (see Figure 1). This increases the overhead costs of the company but should also increase the production. As the company grows after this

> quote from the field
>
> "*T*he lead carpenter system has sped up job production, reduced errors, and increased client satisfaction."
>
> **BRYAN ZOLFO**
> **Insignia Kitchen and Bath**
> **Barrington, Illinois**

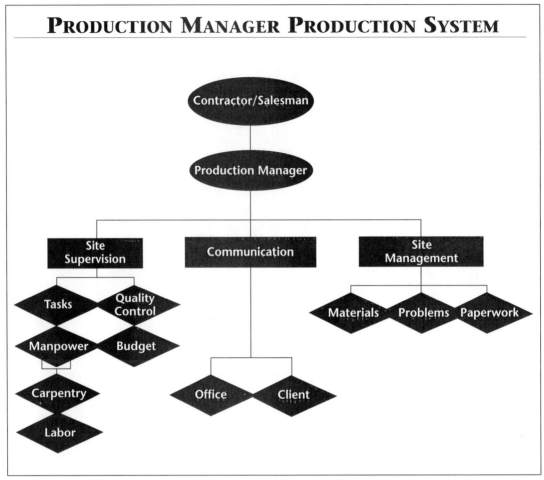

PRODUCTION MANAGER PRODUCTION SYSTEM

Contractor/Salesman

Production Manager

Site Supervision — Communication — Site Management

Tasks · Quality Control

Manpower · Budget

Carpentry

Labor

Materials · Problems · Paperwork

Office · Client

Figure 1. In the traditional approach, when a company grows large enough to run multiple jobs, the contractor hires a production manager to allow him more time to generate sales and manage the business side of the business. The production manager typically travels from job to job to keep production on track and troubleshoot problems.

point, more and more production managers are added to accommodate the increase in work.

Another way, of course, is the lead carpenter system, where a carpenter on the job also fills supervisory and management roles (Figure 2). In this system, the lead carpenters perform essentially the same supervisory role as the production manager, but do this directly on the job site. This tends to be more efficient since most job-site problems can be handled immediately right on the job. There is no down time waiting for a question to be answered from the main office or for the production manager who may be off on another job. Also there is no down time for the supervisor—when he's not performing management tasks, he's swinging a hammer.

When a company grows large enough and is running large numbers of concurrent projects, it may need a production manager in addition to its

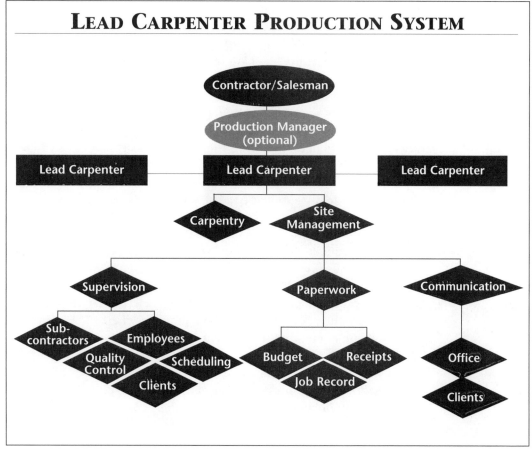

LEAD CARPENTER PRODUCTION SYSTEM

Figure 2. In the lead carpenter approach, supervisory responsibilities are pushed down to the job site through the lead carpenters. This reduces down time since problems that arise on the job can be handled efficiently and effectively on the job site. With multiple lead carpenters, some companies find the need for a production manager as well to maintain effective communications and control.

lead carpenters. However, this system still retains the efficiency and effectiveness of the lead carpenter system.

OLD ASSUMPTIONS, NEW REALITIES

As you can imagine, not every contractor is instantly ready to turn over key management responsibilities to lead carpenters. This prospect raises a number of questions: Can a carpenter effectively supervise a job? Will a carpenter want to assume this level of responsibility? I propose that these concerns were once valid, but that most carpenters of today are very different from those of yesterday, as I'll explain below. Therefore, the production systems typically in place today, which are based on the old reality, may need to be reconsidered. Here are the old assumptions and the new realities:

Old Assumption: *Carpenters don't want responsibility.*
New Reality: *Carpenters come to remodeling from many different backgrounds, and many* do *want responsibility.*

More and more carpenters have tried running their own businesses, as I did, and decided they were not cut out for running the whole show. But, like me, they like some responsibility. Plus, many are college educated and worked summers in construction to get through college. Unable to find a job in their field, they turned to the trade and brought with them a wide variety of experiences, including the ability to learn and master many ideas at a time. This type of contractor possesses a strong desire to be successful.

Some carpenters tried their hand at another profession, found no personal satisfaction, and so turned back to the craftsmanship of construction. These people have chosen construction, and are therefore motivated to learn and make it work for them. They also understand what it is like to be emotionally invested in their work and the need to make it succeed.

Although there are still people who simply want to show up, work, and go home (and it's important to identify those and not try to turn them into lead carpenters), I believe the days are gone when all or even most carpenters are content with that mentality.

Old Assumption: *Carpenters can't serve as supervisors.*
New Reality: *As I mentioned above, people come to construction from many different backgrounds, and increasingly come with the ability to manage people.*

Thirty years ago, most carpenters came into the trade right out of high school, or even before that. Today, a greater number of people attend college and spend their college years working part-time in restaurants, retail stores, and other types of businesses, often in low-level managerial positions.

One carpenter I know worked for years as a staff member at a Boy Scout camp, supervising the staff, which provided him hands-on experience dealing with people in a work environment. Another lead carpenter I know came out of many years of church ministry, bringing with him good people skills. Others have received formal training while working for McDonald's or Burger King. Some have even anticipated a career in the trades and have received formal construction management training on a college level. You would have been hard pressed to find someone like that decades ago.

In addition, these carpenters are generally older when they hear about the opportunity to be a lead carpenter. Age brings maturity and life experiences that help with this job. Age can also bring stabilizing influences such as marriage and children. These life experiences often give people skills in managing many responsibilities at one time, as well as in conflict resolution.

Old Assumption: It is not profitable for carpenters to spend time supervising.

New Reality: The age of TQM (total quality management) has helped us understand this: By bringing everyone into the process of running the job, we produce a better product at a better profit.

More minds tackling the same problem or task produce a better result, as in the old saying "two heads are better than one."

Fresh ideas and fresh approaches help move the company forward. In the new approach, each person on the job has responsibility for the finished product. And responsibility produces ownership, ownership produces pride, and pride produces a better overall product. If everyone in the company has a stake in the success of the company, success is more likely to be achieved.

And, of course, having a trained supervisor at the point of the work—the job site—leads to fewer mistakes and fewer callbacks. And as you know, this is a tremendous money saver.

Old Assumption: We are selling a product.

New Reality: Finally, we have begun to realize that we are not selling just new siding or more space, but service.

People today expect high levels of service. The Disneys, Wal-Marts, and Nordstroms of this world have set a standard by which all of us are being judged. The question to ask is: Who delivers that service? When you go to Wal-Mart, who greets you? Not Sam Walton. Not the marketing department who brought the customers in. It's the front-line people.

In a remodeling company, the salesperson (often the contractor) promotes and sells the service of improving a client's home. The ads are published, the potential client comes in, site visits are made, and a contract is signed. At this point the expectations are very high. The clients are expecting Disneyland service. Who will deliver that service? The front-line employees. I believe that the lead carpenter system, with the lead at the head of the service team, has the best chance of delivering that level of service.

Old Assumption: All types of construction require the same type of supervision.

New Reality: Luckily, we have come a long way toward understanding that different types of construction require different approaches to management.

We cannot use the same style of management in high-rise construction as in new homes, and we can't use the same style in new homes as in remodeling. As I mentioned in the Introduction, there are major differences between building a new home and remodeling an existing home that affect the management style required for that process. The lead carpenter system provides the constant attention that is required by the complex conditions in a remodel.

KEY RESPONSIBILITIES

Here is a brief synopsis of how the system can work in your company (I'll discuss each part in more detail in later chapters):

Core responsibilities. Not every lead carpenter carries the same set of responsibilities. However, most share some basic core responsibilities:
- Plans the job
- Establishes daily work tasks
- Determines daily labor needs
- Supervises all on-site labor
- Maintains job-site paperwork
- Schedules and supervises subs
- Orders and receives materials
- Collects and collates time sheets
- Resolves small plan discrepancies
- Estimates and approves small change orders (up to $500)
- Handles routine customer relations
- Oversees job-site safety
- Prepares punch list

Optional responsibilities. Other aspects of the job description vary depending on the specifics of the company, the job, and the individual lead.
- Collects payment for work completed
- Holds regularly scheduled client meetings
- Grants subcontract bids
- Follows up on warranty callbacks
- Runs the preconstruction conference

Job Planning

Setting up the job is the most critical stage of the project. In the lead carpenter system, this is done by the site manager — the lead carpenter. In other systems it may be done by the salesman or the owner.

The lead carpenter spends some time reviewing all the documents of the job and the site itself to see if all the information he needs has been provided. He checks to see that the specs are clear and the estimate makes sense, and that the plans and the specs agree. He develops a schedule and notifies subs about the schedule. This type of overview checking is a vital step that is all too often overlooked in the interest of "getting started."

Performing Carpentry and Supervising Others

The lead carpenter is responsible for all the carpentry work and other trades' work if the company performs other trades with its own staff. It is his responsibility to assign tasks to other employees on the site, to ask for more help when needed, and to ask that workers who aren't needed be placed on other jobs. Most of these decisions will be based on physical need and budget constraints.

Scheduling and Supervising Subs

The lead carpenter decides when the subs need to be on the job and what they are to do. It is important that the lead be making this decision because he is the only one who really knows how each stage will proceed on the job. The lead must be able to tell the sub what needs to be done, when it needs to be started, and when it needs to be completed.

Job site office. *A corner somewhere on the site can be set up as a portable office—a place for the lead to organize the job-site paperwork and make phone calls.*

First-Line Client Feedback

The lead carpenter is the first person the client will encounter each day who is a representative of your company. He is the person the client talks to about changes, the schedule for the job, and other concerns.

Maintaining Paperwork

The lead carpenter is the person responsible for maintaining all the necessary job-site paperwork. He should not have to maintain all the paperwork, but only what is necessary for someone on the job to fill out or turn in. Receipts, sub bills, job logs, time cards, and schedules are some of the key pieces that might be included. It is important for the contractor to give the lead only the paperwork that is best done by him. Too much paperwork can reduce efficiency.

TEAMWORK WITH SALES

Once the sale is made, it is the salesperson's responsibility to turn over a complete package to the lead carpenter. This includes an estimate, specs, plans, subcontract bids, and all other information the salesman has. If the sale is not complete, i.e., some decisions still need to be made, the salesman must follow up on these as soon as possible. This information should be documented in paper form with dates by which each decision must be made. This allows the lead carpenter to know that he will have the information when he needs it.

Also, the salesman must remain active in the project. The client will be uneasy if the person who sold them the project simply disappears, especially if that person is the owner of the company. The involvement should be just enough to do the following:

- keep the salesman/owner informed of the progress;
- keep the client happy;
- provide input about actual field conditions so that the salesman can be more accurate the next time he sells a job; and
- involve the salesman in the "selling" of change orders as needed.

The contractor/salesperson must be available as back up for the lead carpenter if he needs help with the client or with the project. In reality, the lead carpenter is not left out on his own but has the support of the contractor to produce the project.

For example, a situation may develop where a client wants to change the layout of the windows so that they face a different direction. The lead carpenter can help him to see if this will work structurally and perhaps how much it will cost, but the aesthetic decision should be left to the person who designed the project, whether an architect or designer. Or perhaps a client believes that the whirlpool tub that he had talked about with the salesman at their first meeting is still part of the contract, but the lead carpenter can't find it in the specs or plan. The salesman must get involved to help figure out whether it's in or out. Was there was a verbal agreement on particular items, such as a solid door in one location and hollow doors everywhere else? (We all know that no one ever makes verbal agreements, but for the sake of illustration we will allow one here!) The salesperson will have to be involved to corroborate the client's view.

This is the concept of teamwork. The salesperson provides to the lead carpenter everything that he can to allow the carpenter to produce a job. The lead then turns around and works diligently to bring the job in on the budget set by the salesperson. What happens if the salesperson makes a mistake? The lead does his best to cover for that. What happens when the lead makes a mistake? The team pulls together to work out how it can be corrected. It is important to communicate about these things so that mistakes can be avoided in the future, but it is also important that the communication not be accusatory finger pointing. Remember, all the players have tough jobs.

Mindset of the Contractor

Moving away from the traditional approach of management and towards the lead carpenter system can be a major adjustment for company owners. Most remodeling companies start small and grow, and the pattern established in these companies is for the contractor to have his hands in everything—sales, production, bookkeeping, and marketing. A contractor likes this control. He likes knowing what is going on every day in every aspect of the company. In short, people who start companies and make it past the first five years are the glue that holds it all together. As the company grows, however, they realize that they can not be everywhere at one time and begin looking for ways to bring in others to help with the load. When considering the lead carpenter system as part of this move, it is important for the contractor to understand how this will affect the company and himself.

For the whole system to work, the contractor must be able and willing to do things differently than before.

Accepting Ideas From Others

One of the benefits of this system is that the company has more than one person working on solutions to the problems that plague remodeling. The lead carpenter is actively trying to determine the best solution and will often achieve better solutions than the contractor will simply because he sees the job from a different perspective.

Delegating Control

As we all know, giving up control is very difficult, even painful. The complaint heard most often from carpenters is that the contractor is "always looking over my shoulder." The complaint heard most often from contractors is "how come it's taking so long?" The contractor must establish trust between himself and the lead carpenters so that the leads can be left to do their job, or the system won't achieve its full potential.

Sharing Information

Control of information is power. And in our competitive world we feel the need to control information heavily. In this system of management, the contractor is turning a job over to a carpenter and asking him to produce it at a profit. Every contractor should ask this question: What do I need to be able to produce this job at a profit? The obvious answer is: Everything! This includes budgets, bidding strategies, pricing formulas, contracts, specs, etc.

To ask the lead carpenter to successfully produce a job, and only give him the address of the house, is ridiculous. It is equally ridiculous to ask him to meet a budget but not give him the budget and some idea of how you got there. Information is the key to running a good company. It is also the key to running a profitable job. The contractor must share information with people in the field, specifically the lead carpenters.

Training People

Many carpenters come to a remodeling company with proficiency in crafting wood into beautiful objects. They can create miters that will not separate. They can build a cabinet that belongs in a museum. They can frame a 30-foot wall within $\frac{1}{16}$th of an inch. But they have never produced a job from start to finish. The ability to manage people, understand the budget, follow the paperwork, and relate to clients are all traits that have to be learned. To make it more complicated, these are tasks that usually have to be relearned in each company, because each company does them differently. It is the responsibility of the contractor to provide training for his carpenters to enable them to do their job. I have often complained about the inability of a carpenter to perform a task only to realize later that he had never been trained to do it a certain way. This training will take time, of course, but it's worth the effort once someone becomes trained in your company's ways.

Pay for the expense of training people. There is a trend developing in the building industry to provide training for carpenters. There has always been training available for carpentry skills, whether on the job or apprenticeships. But now through the efforts of some trade associations, publishers, and individuals, real training is available in job management skills. I recently ran an all-day seminar for lead carpenters where 175 people with eager faces packed the room. All of this training costs money, but can produce real results. Seminars of this type walk carpenters through a job and discuss the management aspects of it. Trade magazines regularly run articles that focus on these skills. There are at least three major conferences that provide such training seminars as well as the opportunity for carpenters to interact with other carpenters. Local trade associations offer these same opportunities.

Fire people who don't want to be trained. It is important, when discussing turning over key portions of the business to carpenters, that the contractor have in place good employment practices. This includes the proper procedures for hiring and firing people. Chapter 5 covers this in more detail.

It is easy to hire people, but more difficult to fire them. In the case of lead carpenters, if you end up with a person that does not fit the job description or does not want to be trained to the job, it is essential that they be let go. Keeping a lead carpenter on board who is not working out can be very frustrating for the contractor. There is potential for losing a lot of money. The employee can poison the attitudes of others in the company, even destroy a company. And the contractor can become convinced that the system does not work and lose out on some great growth potential.

Providing Job Descriptions

In order for this system to work, everyone in the company must have a clear and concise job description. In the past, the contractor has always been there to tell people what tasks he wanted each to do. In this system, lead carpenters are out there on their own and need clearly defined responsibilities. This applies to all people in the company: the contractor, the secretary, the carpenter, the truck driver, and the laborer. Once the job descriptions are written, they should be shared with everyone so that everyone knows who should be doing what.

When the Job Loses Money

Every contractor has lost money on a job. Often this loss is because of something that he did or failed to do in the planning process. We all accept this as part of doing business. But it is a harder pill to swallow when the contractor leaves the decision making to a lead carpenter, and the job loses money. The fault may still lie with the estimate or the planning, but the tendency is to lay it all at the feet of the field personnel. Worse still, the fault may lie with the lead carpenter. It is important that the contractor be able to deal with these kinds of situations in a rational manner.

Managing and Valuing Employees

There has been a tendency in construction to view field people as expendable commodities. Contractors will need a carpenter, so they place an ad, hire someone, work him on a job and then fire him when it's done. To make the lead carpenter system work, however, the company must make a commitment to the employee and the employee must make a commitment to the company. Contractors must be willing to learn good management skills: how to train, reprimand, listen to complaints, and do long-range planning so that employees feel secure. These skills do not come naturally to the carpenters-turned-contractors, and must be learned.

MINDSET OF THE LEAD CARPENTER

The mindset of the lead carpenter is, of course, critical to the success of the program. Besides having good craft skills, the lead carpenter must possess many other skills as well.

Interpersonal Skills

Typically, in the standard system, if the carpenter on a job has a problem working with the homeowner or a subcontractor, he can simply be moved to another site. In the lead carpenter system, that is no longer an option. This person must be able to work effectively with all types of people and handle the stress that comes from dealing with a wide range of personalities. There are people who yell a lot, people who come unprepared for work, people who don't work at all, people who don't seem to take anything seriously, people who take everything too seriously, and the list goes on.

Organizational Skills

It may be unrealistic to ask that people be organized in all parts of their lives, but a lead carpenter needs this asset as it relates to a construction site. The ability to stay abreast of everything that needs to be done, and be able to look ahead and plan for tomorrow, is essential. This trait is often evident in the way carpenters keep their tools. Are their tools organized or thrown around? What is the condition of their truck, particularly the dashboard? Keeping track of costs, memos, orders, and change orders is vital to the success of the job. All of this requires organizational skills.

Open-Minded Attitude

The ability to be trained is critical to the long-term success of a lead carpenter. He must be willing and able to learn new ideas and concepts. Many of these people will be coming out of traditional companies with traditional systems of management and will find this system very odd. They will need to learn new tricks. Nothing will stop a system dead in its tracks like people who refuse to try something new. One clue is a person's educational background; someone who is a high school or college graduate has demonstrated an ability to learn.

Great Communication Skills

This includes an ability to express ideas clearly to people in the trades, as well as to people not in the trades. This person will be the primary contact point for clients. Will he be able to address their concerns and answer their questions in a way that will aid the company?

Team Player Outlook

In the lead carpenter system there is a lot of interaction between the sales staff, contractor, lead carpenter, clients, helpers, etc. Very seldom does everyone do everything right. Is the lead carpenter willing to shoulder some of the responsibility for mistakes that others have made and continue to produce to the best of his ability? Is he able to help make this a team effort? This is much like a sports team. If one person misses a tackle, all the others have to put out a little harder to make up for it. They do this because it is a team sport and they know that they will all miss one sooner or later—and someone else will cover for them.

Optimism and Adaptability

Remodeling work is challenging, as you know, and a good lead carpenter must be able to roll with the punches. The lead carpenter cannot afford to adopt an attitude like "this is the job from hell" and let this affect his work. He must be able to see the glass as half full, not half empty.

In addition to this optimistic attitude, he must be adaptable. He will be working with changing schedules and people, and must be able to keep his cool when things don't go exactly as planned.

COMMUNICATION: THE KEYS TO THE KINGDOM

Because the lead carpenter system introduces another person into the mix of who is responsible for a remodeling project, clear and precise communication between the players can make or break the system, as well as your business.

In the system of management typically used in a smaller or emerging company, the contractor doesn't have to find out what's going on from someone else; he is involved all the way through the job.

But with the lead carpenter system, communication must be addressed. Systems must be put into place and understood by everyone so that information moves smoothly from one part of the company to another, from the office to the job site, and to the contractor and back again.

Passing the baton. *The preconstruction meeting is an important step early in the remodeling project where the contractor or salesman introduces the clients to the lead carpenter and passes control of the job.*

In general, three primary tools are used to facilitate this communication—effective meetings, forms, and verbal communication. All three are dealt with at length later in the book, but I mention them here because of their importance. If you don't deal carefully with this facet of the lead carpenter system, or don't intend to, you may as well stop reading this book now and stick with your current system of management.

Effective Meetings

The first critical method of communication is effective meetings. In the first meeting, all the information the salesperson has that relates to the job is turned over to the lead carpenter. This is often called "passing the baton" or a "turnover meeting." This meeting will set the stage for the pattern of communication throughout the entire job.

The next hurdle—weaning the clients from the salesperson and connecting them with the lead carpenter—is accomplished at a preconstruction meeting. The carpenter then begins formal or informal meetings with the clients on the site in order to keep them informed of the progress of the job, to discuss decisions that need to be made, and to give or receive other important information. At the same time, communication must continue to flow from the carpenter to the office, and from the office to the field. This can be done with meetings on the site with the salesperson, production manager, or contractor. It is important to note that meetings are a tool that should promote productivity, not hinder it. Meetings, therefore, should be run in a controlled and effective fashion to make the best use of everybody's time.

Forms

The second type of communication—forms—is an excellent way to get information from one part of the company to another, and to outside vendors. Plus, forms provide a written "paper trail" of the job, which can be valuable if questions arise later. Like poorly run meetings, forms can become a waste of valuable production time if they are not well thought-out. Site communication forms—which are simple duplicate pages that the lead carpenter and contractor can use to write notes to each other —can promote communication on the site. Schedules and lists communicate expectations for the job and the week. Job logs communicate the conditions on the site and the daily progress of the job. But remember that forms must be simple and useful in order to aid in the process. (You will find many excellent forms throughout this book and in Appendix A.)

Verbal Communication

The third communication method is verbal, whether in person or via voice/fax/e-mail. Technology has helped us out here, and pagers, cell phones, fax machines, telephones, and e-mail are all forms of communication that give us instant contact with a site, the office, or the clients. Every company should evaluate its needs and provide the technology it needs to stay in touch. A little investment can go a long way toward effective communication, and toward the success of your company.◣

A Typical Day in the Life Of a Lead Carpenter

What does a lead carpenter actually do over the course of a day? If you stand back and observe a lead carpenter working, what would you see? Of course, not all lead carpenters will do exactly the same things, and they certainly will not perform every function every day the job is in progress. But let's take a bird's-eye view of how a lead carpenter's day might go. (Actually, we've made it a very complex day, to show you a larger number of situations where the lead takes the lead.)

Administration First

The lead (let's call him "Larry" for our story) arrives on the job 15 minutes before the start of the work day. His first function is to check the daily "to-do" list. (This list is generated from the schedule and is basically notes that break the schedule down into small concrete tasks. At the end of each day, the lead generates the to-do list for the next day.)

The items on the to-do list, which Larry completes in half an hour, call for him to do the following:

(1) assign other employees to tasks;

(2) schedule the plumber and electrician to rough in the job two weeks hence, and have the plumber stop by to discuss layout and preparation;

(3) order material for the deck; and

(4) check with the office on a discrepancy between the plans and the specifications. One of the subs is unavailable, so Larry sets up a time to call him back.

Production Begins

With his administrative duties out of the way, Larry turns to production. Today's schedule calls for the framing and sheathing of the roof. The two people assisting him (Jennifer and Tom) have the cords, tools, and equipment out and are ready to roll. A short (five-minute) planning meeting to explain the daily schedule helps all employees know what they are trying to accomplish that day. In this case, Tom will carry 2x10s from the front of the house to the addition, and start cutting rafters. Jennifer will bring the skylights around and build the right sized headers so they can be installed when needed. While this is being done, Larry will lay out the ridge for rafter locations and skylight openings.

(continued)

Here Comes the Client

While Larry figures out how the two rooflines meet, the client (let's call him "Charlie") appears in his bathrobe. He's been looking over the plans and wants to know if the crew can move the window in the far wall about 2 feet to the left to allow room for the couch he and his wife bought the night before. Besides the design, cost, and timing issues of such a change, Larry has another problem; if he stops to chat with Charlie, the crew will shortly be standing around, costing the job money. Larry politely asks for, and Charlie consents to, a meeting in 1 hour.

Impromptu Training Needed

Immediately a new problem arises: it turns out that Tom, who was hired just three days ago, has never laid out or cut a rafter before. A few minutes spent training this new employee results in long-term growth for the job and the company. While doing this, Larry takes the time to check the cords, saws, and work space to be sure there are no safety hazards. One of the cord ends is missing a ground post, so he instructs Tom to fix that before he begins his cutting.

Change Order Needed

By now, the ridge beam is laid, Jennifer and Tom begin setting rafters, and it's time for the client conference. Larry and Charlie look over the plans. They look at the floor plan, the elevations, and the details to detect any conflicts. There appear to be none. Larry tells the client there will be an additional cost for moving the window, but that he can't take the time now to figure it out. He says he will leave it at the "communication station" so Charlie and his wife can review it that night. (Note: During the preconstruction conference, Larry and the clients agreed to post notes and info on a small bulletin board in the kitchen that they called the communication station. This helps them stay in touch, even when they don't see each other for days.) To document that the client initiated the change, Larry writes it up on a "field change order," which he asks Charlie to sign. This form will be forwarded to the office to become a permanent record of the change.

More Production Time

Larry works with Jennifer and Tom to frame the roof. Tom has been cutting rafters, so he continues as Jennifer and Larry nail them in place. The layout is working well.

Here Come the Subs

The plumber (Pete) shows up to review the layout of his work. Larry leaves Tom and Jennifer to continue working while he reviews with the sub the layout of the waste pipes and venting. Because Pete will be sending a mechanic to actually do the work, he and Larry mark the location of pipes. And it's a good thing they checked it in advance because a floor joist is in the way of a toilet flange. Larry has some work to do before the mechanic shows up.

Break Time

It is now time for the 15-minute break that the company allows in the morning for safety and for convenience. Larry sees that they are at a good stopping point and he would like to run the window change by the designer (either in-house or independent), to be sure he is not missing something. The break is a good thing; good for morale and good for production. But Larry knows that every minute wasted is lost profit. At 10:15 break time is over. It's everyone back to work until lunch.

Receiving a Delivery

After lunch, the rest of the day moves on without a hitch. At 2 p.m., a delivery comes for the exterior trim. Larry checks it over, comparing it to his order list and the delivery ticket, and signs the ticket. As the roof is going up, the crew discovers that the existing house is a little out of level. This will throw the cornice work off a little so Larry decides to adjust the framing layout a little to be sure it looks right when finished.

End-of-the-Day Duties

By 3 p.m., the crew has accomplished the work for the day and Larry tells them to move the remaining lumber and clean up the site. His job is to prepare for the next day. A quick check of the schedule (the to-do list) tells him that tomorrow is set aside for beginning exterior trim. However, the lumberyard did not include the finish nails that he needed. He figures he will need the nails by about 10 a.m. so he calls the yard to see about a quick delivery first thing in the morning. No luck. Perhaps, Larry says, because Tom lives near the lumberyard, he can swing by on his way to work and pick up the nails. Tom agrees. Larry could do this himself but it will cost less for Tom to do it.

Looking Ahead

Larry also knows that now that the framing is done he will want fewer workers in order to manage the flow of work better and be more efficient. He will have subs working inside and he will be working outside. How many people does he need to effectively work on the exterior trim? His inclination is to keep everyone, thinking that three can always work better than two or one. So he checks his budget. How much money does he have in labor to complete the trim?

(continued)

By doing this, he uses the budget to decide how to make the best use of his labor. He knows that Jennifer has been with the company for a while and is paid more than Tom. Can he use Tom and cut his labor costs? Or should he go for the experience and keep Jennifer? The budget should control this decision. He decides that somebody scrimped on the exterior trim budget and he can only afford to have himself and Tom there to do that work. So Larry calls the contractor or production manager to try to find a place for Jennifer to work the next day.

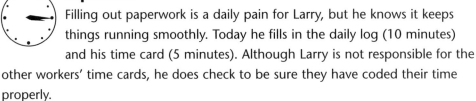

Paperwork

Filling out paperwork is a daily pain for Larry, but he knows it keeps things running smoothly. Today he fills in the daily log (10 minutes) and his time card (5 minutes). Although Larry is not responsible for the other workers' time cards, he does check to be sure they have coded their time properly.

While Larry was at first a bit skeptical about becoming a lead carpenter, he now finds it a very satisfying (and profitable) position, and ends up each day feeling accomplished. With the paperwork done, the site clean, and the doors locked, Larry heads for home at 3:30 p.m.

Chapter 2

Pros, Cons, and Objections Answered

OVER THE YEARS, I'VE GIVEN MANY SEMINARS ON THE LEAD carpenter system and have spoken to many people from companies that were considering this approach. In talking with these contractors, I've noticed that they typically ask the same types of questions and share similar concerns.

In this chapter, I'll address these concerns, looking at both the pros and cons of the system, along with specific strategies to compensate for the problem areas. Like any management approach, the lead carpenter system is no panacea and will have both positive and negative aspects when you try to implement it.

In this system, there are essentially three parties to consider: the contractor, the lead carpenter, and the client. For each party, there are both benefits and drawbacks. The idea is that if you know where the weak points are in the system, you can strengthen those areas of your own operation. And if you know where the system excels, you can focus on that to sell the system and your company's superiority to your carpenters and to your clients.

> quote from the field
>
> *"We mention the lead carpenter system in our sales presentation. We think having a familiar face on the job all the time is a selling point."*
>
> **MIKE CORDONNIER**
> **Production Manager**
> **Remodeling Designs, Inc.**
> **Dayton, Ohio**

BENEFITS FOR THE CONTRACTOR

Growth With Good Service

Loss of good service is one of the biggest fears remodeling contractors and small custom builders have when growing their companies. They feel that their clients have come to expect a specific level of service that only they can deliver. Many remodelers believe that if they begin to leave the job site to tend to the business of selling, or any other aspect of running the business, the service to the client will suffer. The result of this fear, as you may know from personal experience, is that small contractors are so overworked, tired, and stressed out that they never achieve the growth that they want in their business or their incomes.

The answer could be the lead carpenter system, which transfers the construction and management aspects of a job to a person on the site. If the contractor is in the habit of scheduling and meeting all the subcontractors when their work is to begin, he could pass this responsibility over to his lead carpenter. This frees up his time. If the contractor is accustomed to being on the job at 7 a.m. to discuss the progress of the job with the homeowner, the lead carpenter can do that, giving the contractor time for other functions, like writing a business plan, selling more work, "packaging" a job more completely, or perhaps dealing with other problems. Running a business cannot be done on the fly and requires time to plan and act independent of the confusion of daily site work.

Leisure Time

If you are scratching your head and asking yourself, "What is leisure time?" read this section carefully. Working a 40-to-50-hour week in this business is about as common as a two-headed calf. It happens, but it's rare! With a carefully implemented lead carpenter system, a remodeling contractor can have more time to enjoy a personal life (a spouse, children, hobbies, sports, community service, church involvement, and recreation).

With remodeling becoming a recognized industry and people staying in it longer, this is an increasing need. There are families to consider and longevity of the business. It is not unusual for a remodeler to work in the field all day and then do estimates, budgets, etc. in the evenings. The job of running a remodeling company can either control a person or the person can control the process. Hiring capable people to do different aspects of the work is part of controlling the process. If the contractor needs help with sales, the natural thing to do is hire a salesman. If the need is money management, he hires a bookkeeper or accountant. If the need is to get out of the field and enjoy life, hire a lead carpenter. The contractor can attend a baseball game, take a two-week vacation, volunteer on a church committee or charity, sleep in (that might be stretching it!), or do whatever he needs on a personal level.

Better Communication, Better Product

The truth is, better communication with the client can be achieved with the lead carpenter system. There are several reasons for this. The first is that, regardless of the contractor's technical skill, there are always others that can do the job as well as him or better. Secondly, we have to consider the project as a whole. By allowing one person to focus consistently on the project, we obtain a better package. The success of the project is not just in the details of the finished trim, but in the process. Was someone there when the client wanted to discuss the details? Was someone there to clean up when the plumber turned the water back on and the pipe broke? Was someone there to put down plastic, cover the furniture, and close the HVAC return before the drywall was sanded? Those are the details that make a successful project.

With the lead carpenter system, you have somebody on the job site whom a client can go right up to and say, "Bob, why does this room look smaller here than it does on the plans? Are you sure it's the right size?" Instead of having to call someone who's in a meeting somewhere and wait for the answer to come back, the lead carpenter can get the tape out and say, "Yes, ma'am, it's 14 feet 6 inches, just like the plans call for. I know it looks small now, but you'd be amazed at how it's going to look when the drywall goes up! And that window you've added over here to bring in the morning light will really look good too!"

On-the-job management. *With a lead carpenter on the site from start to finish, the client always has someone available for questions. This makes for great customer service and a better product.*

The job looks like it's always running—it is—and that leads to a happier client. With the crew-type system, you have several different subs coming in for different phases and there are gaps in the process. So sometimes clients think that you have left them or worry because nothing is getting done. But when you have one person on the job from beginning to end whom they can communicate with, they know something is happening every day and they end up happier. Remember, we are selling a service, not just a product.

Increased Profits

Because the bottom line is the critical part of the equation, it is important to see how the lead carpenter can affect the bottom line. The most obvious way is increased management with little increase in overhead. The addition of a production manager to supervise all the sites and handle the increase in work, for instance, might cost a company $40,000 to $60,000 a year, or more.

For a small company that can't afford to raise its prices, that represents a considerable percentage increase in overhead expense. Unless the company's total volume grows sufficiently to cover the additional overhead, the difference will show up as reduced net profit.

By distributing supervisory responsibility to several lead carpenters, the contractor can keep the increase in overhead to a minimum. Whether he raises wages for lead carpenters or hires less expensive carpenters to make up for the lead carpenter's reduced field production, the contractor spends less than he would to hire a production manager. The sales volume may still have to go up to cover the extra cost, but not nearly as much; and with lead carpenters managing jobs, the contractor will have more time to sell new work.

But it's just as likely that the additional overhead will be offset by increased efficiency. As lead carpenters improve site management—by coordinating labor resources and subcontractors, controlling waste, and reducing the number of expensive mistakes—production costs will go down, more so on bigger jobs.

Finally, labor costs can be controlled with careful training and well-planned incentives throughout this system. Bonuses and incentives will be discussed in Chapter 5, but I will mention here that they can be real motivators for carpenters to actively control spending, particularly in the labor area.

DRAWBACKS FOR THE CONTRACTOR

Distance From the Craft

Perhaps the greatest drawback to a remodeler or custom builder who is accustomed to being in the field is the feeling that he is no longer "creating." Most tradespeople get into the business because they enjoy the process of creating a finished project. A great deal of satisfaction is derived from standing back and realizing that you have made something from nothing. This satisfaction will fade away the further you get from the field.

Solution: Find the satisfaction that comes from creating a well-managed and profitable company.

Conflict of Interest

The relationship that develops between a remodeler or custom builder and a client often becomes friendly, which is one of the nice elements of this business. And this friendliness can lead a contractor to "soften" and "give away" too many things. He has a vested interest, however, in not doing this since his livelihood depends on a fair profit. The same close relationship can develop between the client and the carpenter—indeed you want there to be a good relationship. But, as human nature dictates, this creates a situation where the loyalty of the lead carpenter can shift to the client and he is apt to give away some work. This makes the client happy, but lowers your bottom line.

Solution: Keep a close connection with your lead carpenters through company meetings, company-oriented get-togethers, and even casual lunches. Also, bonus or incentive programs will help the lead carpenter have as much interest in the bottom line as you do.

Loss of Control

Have you ever ridden on the back of a motorcycle? It's very different from driving it yourself. Maybe you have the same feeling in a car when someone else is driving. Many remodelers who are accustomed to being in control will be uneasy or perhaps afraid of the feeling that they have handed control over to someone else.

Solution: Know that this is a common feeling. Find, hire, and train extremely competent lead carpenters who can do it better than you. And if you can't overcome your objections to handing over control, this system of management is not for you.

Someone Else's Mistakes

Occasionally, mistakes are made on the site that cost the contractor money, and sometimes big money. I remember one occasion when a lead carpenter, anxious to take off for a beach trip, left a helper to cover a roof over a long holiday. But the tarp blew off and rain caused about $20,000 worth of damage and nearly damaged a valuable painting as well.

Solution: Who among us is perfect? We have to realize that all of us make mistakes and accept it when it happens. Of course, it's a harder pill to swallow when it is someone else's mistake.

Benefits for the Lead Carpenter

Greater Profits: More Income

Lead carpenters should be paid more than regular carpenters. Taking on responsibilities that the contractor once assumed can provide opportunities for the company to increase earnings. The lead carpenter should get a bite of that. Plus, bonus and incentive programs can bring even more dollars into a good lead's pocket.

Greater Responsibility

Specifically, this means the power of running a job without the liability of running a company. Many of the best lead carpenters I know are people who had their own businesses at one time and for various reasons decided to work for someone else instead. The reason they make such good leads is that they thrive on being in charge; it's just that being in charge of a whole company is too much. They love the interaction, but know that it all doesn't fall on them. They often love the production side

> quote from the field
>
> *"The lead carpenter feels more a part of the company than just an employee banging nails and punching a time card."*
>
> **NAT BEER**
> **N.A.B. Builders**
> **Ottowa, Illinois**

of the company, but not the selling side. In short, being a lead carpenter gives them the opportunity to run the job without all the responsibility that comes with being a business owner.

Greater Self Respect

This comes from seeing a whole project through to the end. There is a great sense of satisfaction with being able to say, "I built that."

DRAWBACKS FOR THE LEAD CARPENTER

Greater Accountability

More responsibility means greater accountability for the lead carpenter. When someone is simply told what to do, he can often deflect criticism by saying: "I was only doing what I was told." The lead carpenter system, however, gives responsibility to the carpenter and that carries more accountability. You can't have one without the other.

Solution: Make sure the carpenter you hire or train to be a lead has the maturity to accept accountability. It takes a big person to say, "I blew it."

Paperwork

Paperwork is the least favorite part of any lead carpenter's job. Most carpenters are carpenters because they want to create, not keep records of what's being created. And a lead's new set of responsibilities will include more time doing paperwork.

Solution: Accept this fact: If someone wants to be a lead carpenter, he will have paperwork to do, sometimes a little and sometimes a lot. You can help by creating paperwork systems that are simple but effective (see Chapter 8). If you want to leave your lead carpenter time to do carpentry, allow the office to handle as much paperwork as feasible.

Dealing With People

Compared to a carpenter, the lead carpenter is much more involved in dealing directly with people. Sometimes this is not so much fun. I remember one time I was talking to a client about the craftsmanship of one of our employees. The client was questioning his skill and experience and telling me what she thought in very plain English, if you see what I'm getting at. When the diatribe was finished, and the client had gone away, a carpenter on the job said, "I wouldn't want your job." As with paperwork, many carpenters don't want to be involved in the sometime tough discussions about changes, money, and problems that arise on every project.

Solution: You need to hire the right people, and you must also train them to manage. Face it, if you try to transform a painfully shy, introverted carpenter into a lead carpenter, you can expect trouble. Either the client will be put off by the carpenter's demeanor, or the lead will quit out of frustration. Hire the right type of person, making sure his communication skills are top notch. One delightful seminar being advertised lately is: "How to Deal with Difficult People." Consider investing $99 and a day's pay in such a seminar to get your lead carpenters up to a high level of competence in dealing with people.

Benefits for the Client

Quick Access to Management

By having the job management right on the site, the client has ready access to the person who knows the status of each aspect of the job. On remodeling jobs, it is not unusual for clients to want to be involved in the everyday decision making. They will come home from work after everyone has left for the day and look around at the progress that's been made. This will raise questions in their minds and they will want someone to talk to. If they think they won't see the production manager until a couple of days later, they may be inclined to pick up the phone and call someone that night. However, if they know that they will have access to the lead carpenter in the morning, they will often hold their concerns until then. It gives them a sense of involvement during this difficult time when it looks like someone has taken over their house.

This front-line contact is also important to the clients because they will get more accurate information. The lead carpenter who does his job well should have a handle on the whole project and know when and why things are happening. Scheduling is important to clients. Many times during my years as a production manager, a client has called to find out what was going to be happening next. This is hard to predict from the company office or a cell phone in a truck. When I was smart, I said to ask the lead carpenter. When I was foolish (and usually wrong), I would venture out to make predictions. The lead, on the other hand, can assure the clients that the job is on schedule, that work is being done, and that the subs will be arriving tomorrow as planned.

A Better Product

The presence of an on-site manager will produce a better product. One reason for this is job ownership. As mentioned earlier, the lead carpenter begins from day one to own the job. This makes the lead want to produce a product that he can be proud of, which inherently produces a better product. This ownership also helps reduce the common practice of leaving some task or problem for someone else to take care of — the "let the painter fix it" syndrome. Rather, a lead carpenter is present consistently through the entire job, and makes decisions early in the project that are carried through to the end.

DRAWBACKS FOR THE CLIENT

Slightly Longer Time Frame

Sometimes it takes a little longer to complete the project, particularly given the fact that at times there will only be one person doing the carpentry work. It won't be double the time or even a third again as much, but it will add extra time. I will address the solution to this below.

Figure 3. A job-site sign can do more than serve as a good marketing tool. If it includes the lead's name, it can reinforce his authority with the client.

Wanting To Deal With the Boss

There is still a perception in mainstream America that if you want something done, you go straight to the top. I have worked with people who wanted to deal only with the boss. These are people who are accustomed to discussing their needs with the principals of whatever organization they are dealing with.

Solution: The lead carpenter must be presented as "the boss" for the project. The contractor can do a lot to help clients view the lead as an authority. For starters, the contractor should let the lead carpenter plan and run the preconstruction meeting. By deferring to the lead as the job progresses, the contractor reinforces the lead's authority. For instance, when a client calls up and starts to ask the contractor questions, he should reply with, "Why don't you ask Larry about that when you see him; I don't really have the answer for you." Or: "Larry is the one who has that information; I'll check with him and have him call you right back." Another idea is to have a job-site sign on the project that states clearly who is responsible on that site (Figure 3).

Note: If the contractor has an overwhelming need to be the most important person in the company in all aspects and isn't willing to support the lead as the job-site authority, this system will not work.

Hard Transitions

If a lead carpenter leaves a company, or must leave the job for an extended period, the clients have a very difficult time making the transition to another lead. When a lot of emotional collateral has been deposited in one lead, it is hard for the clients to trust or work with another lead.

Solution: The only solution is to avoid, with all your power, changing leads in the middle of a job.

POSSIBLE OBJECTIONS ANSWERED

Below are the objections I have heard many times from remodeling contractors considering the lead carpenter system. Each raises a valid concern, but each can be overcome by someone committed to making the system work.

The Clients Want *Me*

In other words, "When I sold the job, I sold myself." The secret is to educate the client from the beginning about how this system, and your company, operate. You explain that at a certain point, you will be turning them over to the capable hands of your lead carpenter, one of the best examples of humanity you've ever met, etc. Let the customer know that you run a company staffed by the best people in the business. However, if somehow you attract only those clients who insist on having the contractor supervise the job, you should not use this system. Another aspect of this objection is the need for training. You can never get someone else to be just like you, but you can hire and train others that will represent you well to the client. And sometimes you can hire and train people that are better than you.

Finding Good People

There are two ways to look at this issue. First: Are there good people out there? I believe the answer is yes. In my company we have been able to find some of the most qualified, most diligent people you could hope for. I'll talk about where and how to find them in Chapter 5, "Hiring and Training." Second, we should admit that we are never going to find anyone that fits our mold perfectly. So we need to train people and nurture them into our ways of doing things. Do you want the company tools maintained a certain way? You'll need to train your employees. Do you want the client's home buttoned up a certain way at the end of the day? Again, training is the key. This is discussed in greater detail in Chapter 5.

Plus, you must have a good company to work for. There must be a friendly, harmonious, albeit hard-working, atmosphere. The pay and benefits must be at the top of the range. And all your systems—training, paperwork, pay raises, etc.—must be in smooth working condition in order to retain top-notch people. Don't expect the best in the field to enjoy working in chaos.

This Way Takes Too Long

I have already conceded earlier that using this system, and embracing the idea of using as few workers on the job as is possible, will cause each project to take a little more time to complete. I've heard this objection before, and I have several responses.

First, the speed of completion is not generally the issue, but rather finishing the job when you promised to finish. If you give clients a good idea of how long it will take, they are usually okay with that. Second, we're not talking about a lot of extra time here. A two-month job, for instance, would not end up being a four-month job. It may be a few days longer. That's because, generally speaking, having more people on a job does not automatically bring more efficiency. If all this is explained early on to clients, they will understand. Third, we must understand that simply running subs through a job or bringing on different crews for different aspects of the job does not necessarily mean the job takes less time. In fact, it can mean more time because of the difficulty of scheduling the subs or the crews.

Sharing Secrets

The thinking is, if I share the budgets and profit margins with my employees, they will want a cut of the pie. Ironically, the key to solving this problem is to share everything with them. Share the budgets, markup, overhead, profit, what you do to make the company work, how jobs are sold, and how much time goes into that, etc. What this should do is help the employees understand how much it really costs to keep the company going and how they fit into that puzzle. On the other hand, keeping them in the dark makes them think that the contractor and the company are making piles of money, while the labor is being cheated. And, if you are making piles of money, please give me a call and let's do lunch. I want your secrets. It's just human nature that everyone will always want more of the money, and good employees should be paid fairly. Helping them understand where all that money goes will only improve the company.

Safety Issues

I advocate using as few people as necessary to build the project, and at times this will mean the lead carpenter is working alone on the job. Consequently, some people raise the objection that one-person job sites aren't safe. While this is a valid concern, it's not insurmountable.

First, I would like to note that safety ought to be a company's concern regardless of the number of people on the site. The company must establish that workers' safety is a top priority and that it is company policy that every person on a job site use safe practices. This is accomplished though regular training and constant reminders about safety. In addition, companies should provide safety equipment as needed and never ask anyone to do something that is unsafe. These policies, by themselves, will reduce the accident rate of any company. And by making it clear that additional people are available when needed, a company can ensure that a carpenter will not try to do a task that really requires more than one person.

Also, a company should provide adequate communication on every job site for both emergency calls and regular calls. An emergency phone list should be by the phone or readily available.

While most tasks performed by a carpenter are not high risk, every task has potential hazard when power tools are being used. But in general, there are safe ways to do the work. For example, working on framing a roof is a hazardous aspect of a job. In most cases this is at least a two-person job. Running the baseboard in an addition could be hazardous, but in general it's a simple safe task that can be accomplished easily and safely by one person.

As you can see, I have a workable answer for every objection. That's because our company has been using lead carpenters for years, and I don't know what we would do without them. But they're all human, and none of them is perfect and none is a clone of me (and I'm not perfect, either, believe it or not). The secret is to discover and elevate the best elements of each lead, and to strengthen any weaknesses you find. The next chapter will explain exactly what your leads will be asked to do, and after that I'll describe the best methods to find and train these most valuable elements of a growing remodeling or custom building company.◣

Safety first. *This lead carpenter is working alone on a roof, but adhering to the company's safety policy—he's using a harness to protect himself from a fall.*

Chapter 3

Progressive Implementation

So where do you start and how do you implement this system? I wish it was as easy as snapping your fingers and finding the system up and running. It is not that easy — but it's not as difficult as it may seem either. Two overall principles should guide implementation. First, nothing happens overnight. And second, every person and every company is different. This chapter gives some basic guidelines for implementing this system into your company (see Figure 4).

PROPER PLANNING

As with any endeavor, good planning is the key to successful implementation. And the first step in planning is to understand that this system involves the whole company. The lead carpenter system will work well only if it's a part of the larger company plan. It will not work to hand more responsibility to the lead carpenter if other systems within the company are not geared to support that transition. Everyone from the laborers to the president of the company must know how the system works and how it will change his work. When using the lead carpenter system, the sales staff will function differently. The production manager will have a different role to fill. The laborers will be answering to a different person.

With this in mind, the best way to make the transition is to get the whole company involved in putting together a plan. It may be unwieldy to have meetings for everyone in the company to talk about this, but everyone should have input at some point in the process. Even if the principals put together the original plan, it's a good idea to get other company members to critique it and offer ideas to make it better match the style of your organization and the personnel. Consensus building is important. It may help to have one lead that is enthusiastic about the sys-

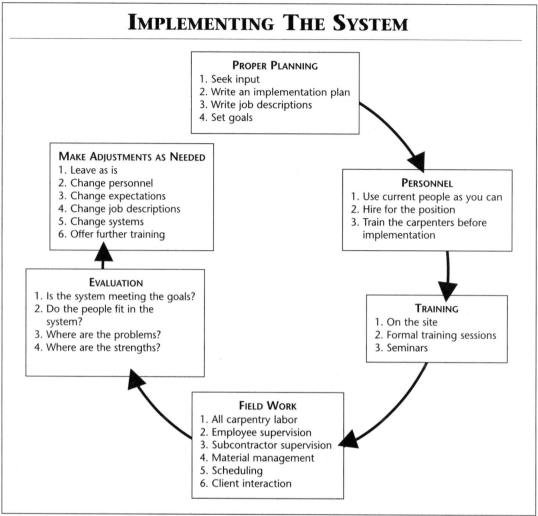

IMPLEMENTING THE SYSTEM

PROPER PLANNING
1. Seek input
2. Write an implementation plan
3. Write job descriptions
4. Set goals

MAKE ADJUSTMENTS AS NEEDED
1. Leave as is
2. Change personnel
3. Change expectations
4. Change job descriptions
5. Change systems
6. Offer further training

PERSONNEL
1. Use current people as you can
2. Hire for the position
3. Train the carpenters before implementation

EVALUATION
1. Is the system meeting the goals?
2. Do the people fit in the system?
3. Where are the problems?
4. Where are the strengths?

TRAINING
1. On the site
2. Formal training sessions
3. Seminars

FIELD WORK
1. All carpentry labor
2. Employee supervision
3. Subcontractor supervision
4. Material management
5. Scheduling
6. Client interaction

Figure 4. Implementation of the lead carpenter system includes specific steps, starting with proper planning and ending with adjusting the system as needed – which may mean circling back to the training phase of the process and moving forward again from there. It's important to view the system as an evolving process.

tem to help others see the possibilities. If the company is large it helps to do this in smaller groups. When you're finished, you will have a better chance of having everyone on board.

Learn From Others

There is nothing like learning from the experience of others, particularly if they are using the system effectively. As you are planning the transition to using this system, seek practical input from an experienced source. Because the system is not rigidly defined, but rather a general concept, you will find that each company has different experiences and uses different strategies to make it work. For some specific examples, see "Four Case Studies" in Chapter 12.

So far, most of the contractors I know who use the lead carpenter system have learned about it either through attending seminars or from talking with other people who use the system, and then they tried to implement it themselves. They have worked at it diligently to iron out the bugs and find the best fit for them. You can easily find such people in your local trade association and learn a lot from their trials and errors. The National Association of Home Builders (NAHB) and the National Association for the Remodeling Industry (NARI) both have members that have been using this system for years. You can also find "experts" at conferences organized by these and other trade groups. Many of the ideas that have changed our company have come from seminars and discussions at various conferences. You can also hire a consultant to come into your company to help develop and implement system. The costs of these ventures are well worth the benefits.

An Implementation Plan

First, write a plan for how you want this system to function in your business. Every business should have a business plan that outlines how the company will grow, what the expected profit is, and who is responsible for what work. The same is true for the lead carpenter system. This plan should be written and tailored to your specific company. It must be written to dovetail with the overall business plan.

Write Job Descriptions

Then, write a job description for a lead carpenter (see examples in Chapter 4). Every carpenter needs a job description. The days are over when we can hire someone over the phone and send him to a job and say, "Just do what you're told."

The job description must have everything in it that you want the lead carpenters in your company to do. If you want them to order the materials, it should be in there. If you want them to run job-site meetings, it should be in there. If they are responsible for installing the job signs, it should be in there. Not only should you write a job description for the lead carpenter, but you should have a job description for every field employee. All of these should relate to the lead carpenter's job description so there is a clear definition of what each person is supposed to do.

And finally, rewrite your own personal job description to include your concept of how a lead carpenter will work with you as the contractor. If you don't have a job description for yourself, this is a good time to write one. This job description is not for you, but for those who work for you. To help you put this down on paper, it may be helpful to ask yourself these questions (and any others you can think of):
• What can the lead carpenter expect from you?
• What are your responsibilities once the job starts?
• When will you step in and make decisions and when will the lead be left to make the decisions?
• When will you be available for consultation?

"If you're going to grow a business of any size, you have to delegate and give control to other people. The lead carpenter situation is the only way to run multiple jobs..."

BILL BALDWIN
Co-Owner
Hartman Baldwin
Claremont, California

It is important that your job description dovetail with the lead carpenter's job description. Again, the purpose of these job descriptions is to define who will do what. One of the biggest fears about this system is that something will get lost in the shuffle or fall through the cracks. The job descriptions can't guarantee this won't happen and won't cover for sloppy work, but they can at least define who is responsible for each part of the work.

Set Goals

Finally, set some realistic goals for yourself to give some structure to the move from paper (the plan and the job descriptions) to the real world. For instance, once you've chosen the right candidates to become leads in your business, what kind of time frame will work for initiating the change? Are you just too busy to put the time into the training and reorganizing because it's summer and you're in the middle of four or five projects? In that case, you may be doing this planning on the side, and will choose to do the actual implementation once fall comes.

Or, you may want to set a goal regarding how many leads you will hire or promote from within in the very beginning. It may work for you to take just one carpenter who works for you and start with him. Or if you've put a lot of planning into this and know you're ready to dive in, perhaps you'll choose to hire on several leads.

FINDING THE CANDIDATES

In looking for candidates to fill this new role in your company, the best place to start is with your current employees. Set up some times to "interview" your employees to see if they want to participate in this system. Evaluate their reactions and decide if you want them to participate. If you have employees who are excited by this plan, you'll know it. They'll be saying things like, "This is great! This should really help us to get the job done better." On the other hand, if you have a worker who feels threatened by change or doesn't like the idea of added responsibility (or suddenly having to answer to a peer who may be promoted to lead), you'll also know it. Negative comments will indicate a negative attitude. This person definitely isn't lead material, and it may even be that he won't work well under a lead once the new system is up and running.

This should be an information session for your employees as well as a fact-finding session for you. You need to explain carefully to your candidates what you are expecting, show them the job description, and answer any questions they have. Be sure you listen very carefully. You will be making a decision about their participation and at what level that will be.

Do not simply ask if they want to be a lead carpenter. Ask the questions that will help you decide if they can handle it. For example, you could ask the following questions:

- How would you do things differently if you were the person solving problems on the site? How would you do things your own way to make a job run better?
- Which additional responsibilities would you like to take while on the site?
- Give me your gut reaction to the term "paperwork."
- Have you ever had a job or been in a situation where you were in charge? How did you like that?

Help wanted. *Candidates for the job of lead carpenter should be extremely well organized. A good lead will have to juggle many responsibilities at once, communicate well, and be able to follow through.*

- How do you feel about moving into a supervisory role, especially regarding those who are currently your peers?
- What kinds of experiences have you had that would help you interact professionally with our clients and our subs?

Remember, as with any interview, it's critical that after you ask the questions you remain quiet and listen attentively. This is the other person's opportunity to tell you about himself— not your time to tell him all about the job.

If you are going to make this change you need to hire people who will fit your needs. If you can't find those people within your own organization, don't throw your hands up and assume the game is lost. Begin interviewing people from outside the company.

Interviewing from outside your company will do several things for you. First, it will acquaint you with the type of people who are available. You may discover, after interviewing outsiders, that the people who already work for you are your best choices for the new position. Or, you may find that you have been settling for second best for a long time. Second, you will refine your ideas about your system. It may be that what you want the lead carpenter to do has to be scaled back, for the time being, until you can bring some people along to your ideal. Third, it may motivate some people who work for you to expand their horizons. Your resolve to make this change may help them commit to working harder to make the company grow. There is nothing like the idea of being replaced to spur some people into action.

TRAINING

Before you implement the system, spend the time and resources necessary to train your people. This could include monthly company meetings, trade journals and newsletters, seminars, trade association meetings, etc. Take the position that anything you want your lead carpenters to do, you must train them to do. This principle applies even when someone comes to you already trained as a lead carpenter. They will have learned a different way of doing paperwork at their former company, for example. Therefore, your training methods must be complete and systematic. Good training has three essential parts: the teaching, the practice, and the critique. Any way that you accomplish the training, it must have these ingredients.

Teaching. Training or teaching can be done in house or out of house or with some combination of the two. In-house training should start with you or someone else on your staff developing a list of the topics for training. The teaching can then be done at meetings, one-on-one settings, or perhaps retreats. If you are a contractor who is in the process of hanging up your belt, training can be done by example on the site. Out-of-house training can be done by consultants or through seminars at conferences and trade shows.

Practice. Practice is a must for all training. The practice takes place as the contractor actually leaves the lead to implement the training. If training is occurring in a meeting, each session must have some practice problem that reinforces the training. For example, if the training is about reading an estimate to see how many hours are available for each task, there should be a problem that is worked into the session so that everyone actually does the work. If training is occurring in a seminar, a follow-up meeting should be held as soon as possible after the training to arrive at specific changes that will be made as a result of the seminar. Each change should have specific actions attached that will be practiced.

Critique. Critique, follow-up, or evaluation must be a part of the training as well. Contractors should never assume that a carpenter has fully understood the training or has followed through with his responsibility to practice the learned skill. There are too many distractions occurring on the job each day that pull carpenters back into the same old way of doing things. The follow-up will depend on the skill being learned but can be handled in a variety of ways. Sometimes a site visit will verify that the carpenter has learned about job site safety. Or a review of his paperwork will confirm that he has learned how important it is to complete it accurately and on time. The important thing is that a skill be learned before another skill is added to the mix.

There are many resources out there for training ranging from books, tapes, and magazine articles to various seminars and workshops. And new ones are emerging all the time. Take advantage of these opportunities and you'll find it's a good investment in your company's success.

INCREASING A LEAD'S RESPONSIBILITIES

- All carpentry labor
- Job schedule and flow of work
- Employee supervision
- Ordering materials
- Subcontractor site supervision
- Informal client contact, such as easy-to-answer questions, change order requests, etc.
- Subcontractor scheduling
- Formal client contact, such as site meetings, change order pricing and selling, etc.
- Negotiating subcontract pricing and scope of work contracts
- Complete control including collecting money, receiving complaint calls, return punch list items, etc.

Note: Each of the above areas carries with it paperwork that the lead must master.

Figure 5. *This is how our company increases responsibilities for a lead carpenter, from simple labor to complete control of a project.*

TAKING IT TO THE FIELD

This is the big step: Taking the system and your plan into the field. Begin with some basics, understanding that not everyone will be able to be—nor should be expected to be—the "ideal" lead carpenter instantaneously. It is a serious mistake to dump all of the responsibilities of the lead carpenter on an individual right away if he is not ready. Start with the pieces that each carpenter can handle and feels comfortable with. If you've decided the six key responsibilities of your lead carpenter are going to be carpentry labor, employee supervision, subcontractor supervision, material management, scheduling, and client interaction, choose one or two which that person already is familiar with (other than the carpentry, of course). You could start with material management and scheduling, for instance, if your new lead is a person who has shown good organizational skills, has already done some ordering for you, and is the one who usually helps receive materials.

Remember, this process may be different for each person. It can be a little confusing at first, but over time people will mature within the system and get on the same track.

Then expand the program as your people can handle it. As the new lead carpenters show the ability to handle each job function, begin adding more and more of the job description to their daily work load until they are doing all of the tasks you want them to do. This may take a couple of years for some carpenters and may take a couple of months for others. It is important to remember that each carpenter will start with different skills so the progression will be different for each. Some will start with ordering their own materials but not scheduling subs. Others will schedule subs but want someone else to order materials. A typical progression is listed in Figure 5.

MODIFY AS YOU GO

Once your new leads are up and running and some time passes, you will probably start to see parts of the picture that are going great and others that aren't working so well. The key is to not quit now even if the program is not working out exactly as you thought it would. Instead, it's time to stand back and take a look at how things are going and then to make the necessary adjustments.

Evaluating The System

Evaluating the system is different than evaluating a carpenter. You will be looking to see if the system has flaws, not whether a carpenter is fitting into the system. The questions you will ask are different. If you're not sure where to start, there are a few basic questions you can ask yourself:

- How well is the system following the plan written at the beginning of the process?
- What were the goals and how well is the system meeting the goals?
- How are the people fitting into the system? How are the leads working out? How are other employees accepting the leads' new role?
- What's working well?
- Where does the system need improvement?

An important part of this process will be to allow the leads in the company to participate in the evaluation of the system. They will give you valuable insight into how it really is working or not working. It may even be best to allow an independent person—someone without a vested interest—to run this meeting so that you receive honest input from the field.

Evaluating the system will involve evaluating the leads. Job evaluations should be done on a regular basis and the interval will depend on your situation. If the system is brand new, you may want to formally evaluate progress every three months. This will allow for adjustments to be made before bad habits become the norm. If the system is up and running, formal evaluations can be done annually. These evaluations should be done in writing and should be based on your job description for the lead carpenter.

Less formal evaluations should be done constantly. These occur at informal site meetings (just dropping by), over the phone (after a review of paperwork), or whenever the need arises. It's been my personal experience that contractors tend to follow two extremes in these evaluations. The first is to evaluate but keep the results to themselves. This leads to frustration for everyone and does not accomplish anything. The second is to criticize rather than critique. This also leads to discouragement and frustration. It is important for contractors to develop ways of evaluating and sharing that information in a way that prompts growth for each lead.

Making Adjustments

Once you've figured out what's working and what's not, you can decide how to make adjustments accordingly. If there is a specific employee who isn't working out, you'll need to decide if it's the employee, the expectations, or just that this employee is valuable in another way. We had a situation where an employee was not a good site supervisor but was a great framer. As we thought about his contribution to the company and the system we decided that he was an asset even though he hadn't met the job description. He was happier and we were happier after we moved him back into a straight production role.

We have also changed our system on many occasions based on input from our leads. There was a time when our leads had to order materials through the office and schedule subs through the office. This led to a lot of frustration for the leads because they never really knew what was happening with the orders or the subs. The leads spoke up at a meeting to ask for that responsibility. They believed it would make the jobs run more smoothly and efficiently. So we handed it over to them. They felt better about their work, we had less to do in the office so we could concentrate on other aspects of the work, we lowered our overhead (the production assistant was no longer needed), and the leads learned how hard it is to schedule deliveries and subs and have them show up on time! But this part of the system was improved.

It should be noted here that making adjustments is a constant event in a company. Every system ever put in place runs down with time. It is a law of nature! So we must always be working on keeping it running well. People will come and go from your company—this will change your system. You will get distracted and focus on selling jobs—the system will slack a little. You will learn something from a book or a seminar that will help you tweak the system a little. All of these events mean that you never stop making adjustments to your system.

A Never-Ending Process

Again, the lead carpenter system is not a rigidly defined set of steps and no two companies will implement it in the same way. Rather it's a concept. So by definition, it will evolve and change as you implement it and decide what works and what doesn't. The hardest part is getting started. From there, if you've planned well and have the right employees, you should start reaping the benefits very quickly. ◢

quote from the field

"At first my partner and I did all the work ourselves... Finally I asked [my best carpenters] to order, schedule, and deal with homeowners. They said "Why didn't you ask us before?"

MIKE CORDONNIER
Production Manager
Remodeling Designs, Inc.
Dayton, Ohio

Chapter 4

Developing A Job Description

THE DAYS ARE QUICKLY FADING WHEN A CARPENTER CAN WALK ONTO A JOB SITE, simply claim he is a carpenter, and begin working. This is especially true for a lead carpenter, and employers around the country are realizing that hiring a lead carpenter should involve not only a job interview, but a check of references, verification of work history, and even testing.

Unfortunately, a key item often overlooked in the hiring process is providing the prospective employee with a clear, concise job description. A written job description is critical for the success of the lead carpenter system because more responsibility is being placed in the employee's hands and there is less direction from supervisors. Employees who are asked to make on-site decisions, suggest improvements, and take more responsibility than ever before need to know which tasks are their responsibility and which ones fall on someone else's shoulders. All of this requires that a clear and complete job description be written for each position. Of course, job descriptions will vary from company to company and from year to year as the company grows and refines its operations.

In this chapter, I'll first show you the lead carpenter job description my company uses, and then the job descriptions used by other companies across the country.

As you'll see, each of these job descriptions is unique, much like every remodeling job is unique. The best way to develop your own lead carpenter job description is to read through these examples, circling the sections you particularly like, and crossing out the items you don't like. In consultation with your partner(s), if any, with potential candidates for the position, and with your own experience and common sense, you'll be able to craft a description that works for your company. And of course, you'll refine the description as time goes by.

JOB DESCRIPTION #1

HOPKINS & PORTER CONSTRUCTION
Potomac, Maryland

Specializing in: . . . . Full Service Remodeling
Number of Employees: 22
Annual Sales Volume: . . . .$3.3 million

Overall Responsibilities
- Customer satisfaction
- Job-site supervision, protection, and cleanliness
- Carpentry labor
- Supervision and scheduling of subcontractors
- Scheduling of inspections
- Material takeoffs and orders
- Maintenance of job-site paperwork

Specific Duties
1. You are the on-site manager for our construction project. Your performance is extremely important to the success of our company. You are our representative to both the client and the community at large. We get most of our work because of our reputation and you are a very important part of that reputation. Both the quality of your work and the appearance of your job site reflect strongly on you and our company.

2. You are responsible for knowing and understanding all job paperwork: Plans, specifications, and change orders. Any questions you have, or discrepancies you discover, should be checked with the project manager. You are responsible for maintaining all job records as required by the office. These records are most important for our work and must be maintained by the lead carpenter.

3. You are responsible for performing all carpentry labor on the job, requesting help as it is needed. When other carpenters or helpers are on your job, you are responsible for assigning them work, expediting their performance and generally supervising them, including expediting their paperwork (time cards, etc.).

4. You will schedule and coordinate all subcontractors, in consultation with the project manager, work out their layout problems, ensure their proper performance and approve their payment, as well as ensure that they get timely inspections on their work. It is your responsibility to be sure that all subcontractors adhere to all of our company's policies concerning safety, cleanliness, alcohol use, and customer satisfaction.

5. The lead carpenter will prepare the final material takeoffs and order materials promptly and accurately. With at least 24 hours notice, we can minimize or eliminate material runs by company employees. All material orders are to go through the project manager to ensure cost control. Carpenters or helpers may pick up materials only under emergency conditions.

You are responsible for accurately checking all materials delivered to your job for quantity and measurement, as well as damage. Delivery truck drivers are to wait for your inspection, as your signature approves the condition and count of the order. Any discrepancy is to be noted on the delivery ticket. It is imperative that you check such things as door swing, window sizes, cabinet sizes and types, lumber type and grade, etc., before you sign the delivery ticket. Remember, it's your job site. (The project manager will be responsible for ordering doors, windows, cabinets, and other "specialty" items.)

6. You must maintain a clean work site. This is important for many reasons, among them safety and efficiency. A sloppy site reflects badly on your work and our company. Dust protection of the client's property is one of your most important jobs. Be sure to control any mud on your site. All job sites are to be broom-cleaned daily. Debris is to be properly stored and hauled away promptly. You must have the client's permission before smoking on the site. It is also your responsibility to monitor smoking by subcontractors on your site as well.

7. You are responsible for the protection of the client's property. Do not use anything, including tools, equipment, or cleaning supplies that belong to the client. Be sure you lock and secure the job site before you leave for the day. You must secure all ladders and equipment on site. All materials are to be stored in a safe place. The client's telephone may be used only with their permission and then only for business or emergency personal calls. You must never disturb a client with loud radios or foul and abusive language.

8. Job safety for both the client and our workers is your responsibility. Be sure that job conditions encourage safety. Monitor both company and individual equipment for proper safety features, safe electrical cords, etc., and inform the project manager of any unsafe conditions. Proper safety equipment must be used when appropriate.

9. We always want to accommodate our client and their wishes but if they want any extra work or make any changes, please refer them to the project manager or to the salesperson. Don't agree to anything without getting approval, and don't ever do work without a change order from the client.

10. You are responsible for installing a job sign in the most prominent place possible and for maintaining its condition. Where appropriate, door hangers or other promotional materials should be distributed in the surrounding neighborhood. Work with the project manager or the salesperson on this; we all benefit when we can sign up new work. Every sales lead is important.

11. The lead carpenter will develop and maintain the project schedule. To be sure your job is on schedule or ahead of schedule, monitor your progress against the flow chart. Notify the project manager as soon as possible of any delays or conditions that will affect the schedule. You must also notify the office if you are having any problems maintaining the schedule. Coordination of all the elements that make up a typ-

ical job requires adherence to a tight schedule. You are our link to the job site and we need to know whether you need any help.

12. Remember, our work day is from 8:00 to 4:30. You and your crew are expected to take a half-hour unpaid lunch. Any deviations from this schedule must be approved by the project manager and by the client. This is best done at the preconstruction conference. We start at 8 a.m. to provide our clients with as little disruption and as much privacy as possible. You are expected to check in with the project manager on a daily basis to report on the progress of subs and inspections, make any manpower requests for the next day, and to discuss materials orders, overall job scheduling, and client concerns.

13. You must pay attention to follow through. Just because you notify the office, a sub, or the client of a question or problem, don't assume someone else is taking care of the situation. It is your job and your responsibility to resolve and complete the loose ends on your job site. The perfect lead carpenter is: Aggressive, Organized, Considerate.

Signature: _____

Date: _____

JOB DESCRIPTION #2

SYLVESTRE CONSTRUCTION
Minneapolis, Minnesota

Specializing in: . . . . .General Remodeling
Number of Employees: . . . . .15, including 6 lead carpenters
Annual Sales Volume: . . . .$1.8 million

Intent:
The responsibility of the lead carpenter is to profitably and efficiently produce remodeling projects using carpentry and management skills.

Overall Responsibilities:
• Produce project as contracted, per SCI standard level of quality and procedure
• Complete projects profitably and on schedule
• Provide customer satisfaction and communication
• Carry out job-site supervision, including protection of property and job-site cleanliness
• Perform all aspects of carpentry labor
• Supervise all subcontractors, carpenters, and laborers on your projects
• Schedule permit inspections
• Perform material takeoffs and quality checks
• Make sure all necessary tools and materials are on your projects
• Maintain all paperwork, including accuracy of time cards

- Be well organized in all aspects of your job
- Have working knowledge of contracts and drawings for all projects you are assigned
- Report to project manager and field supervisor

Specific Duties
- Perform all carpentry labor for job; utilize help as needed
- Coordinate all subcontractors, work out layout problems, and ensure proper performance
- Coordinate materials ordering and delivery: ensure timely delivery, check all job tickets to ensure proper delivery of all items, and coordinate and track returns
- Make timely requests for all necessary inspections, including but not limited to footing, framing, electrical, plumbing and heating, insulation, and final inspections
- Maintain clean and tidy job premises at all times, including dust protection, daily cleanup, organized tool and material storage, weekly trash removal, and final cleanup
- Keep all job records, including time cards, change orders, job communications memo file, material shipping tickets, return tickets, and invoices
- Maintain all personal and company tools
- Participate in preconstruction conference and quality control precompletion punchlist, completing own punchlist
- Interact with customers to ensure their satisfaction
- Have knowledge of labor costs and control throughout the project
- Save all items as directed that are to be reused
- Set clear goals for each worker on site; give clear instructions and confirm that they have been followed
- Protect all of the customer's property
- Be able to lift and use safely all tools and materials necessary in the construction trade
- Be able to lift a minimum of 50 pounds up a ladder to a second-story roof on a continuous basis
- Know all shut-off locations for electrical, gas, water, security, sprinkler systems, etc.
- Set up and maintain job-site safety procedures
- Keep job equipment on site and in good working order
- Be able to work productively at all required working heights
- Perform other job duties and responsibilities as needed and requested by management or immediate supervisor

Skills and Tools Required
- Trade school preferred but not required
- Five years of carpentry experience
- Complete expanded inventory of hand and basic power tools

- Ability to read blueprints, lay out project from foundation up, and follow contract
- Knowledge of basic building code requirements
- Knowledge of basic mechanical requirements
- Ability to perform material takeoffs
- Ability to direct and manage others
- Excellent communication skills

JOB DESCRIPTION #3

> **REMODELING DESIGNS, INC.**
> Dayton, Ohio
>
> Specializing in: . . . . .Kitchens, Baths, Room Additions
> Number of Employees: . . . . .10, including 5 lead carpenters
> Annual Sales Volume: . . . .$1 million

Overall Responsibilities

I. *Extensive General Remodeling Skills*
- Including, but not limited to, painting, tiling, drywall work, carpentry, plumbing, electric, concrete, and all other skills necessary to job completion.

II. *Conduct Job in Safe and Clean Manner*
- Keep job site safe for self and others. Clean site daily prior to leaving for the day.

III. *Communication of Job Progress*
- Keep customer and supervisor informed of job progress on a daily basis.

IV. *Present Self and Remodeling Designs in a Professional Manner at All Times*
- Wear approved uniform (VanDyne Crotty Uniform—shirt and pants) with occasional exception of RDI t-shirt/sweatshirt due to weather. It is employee's responsibility to have clean, well-kept uniforms. Remodeling Designs Inc. uniforms are to be worn only on RDI jobs.
- Loud radios, foul language, and use of customer phones and other conveniences is prohibited.

V. *Scheduling Responsibilities*
- Attend preconstruction meetings with supervisor.
- Schedule and coordinate subcontractors.
- Determine material needs and place orders on a limited basis (e.g., lumber, drywall, plumbing fixtures, etc.).

VI. *Supervisory Responsibilities*
- Assist in interviewing and selecting candidates for carpenter assistant positions when requested.
- Educate and train carpenter assistants when necessary.

- Supervise carpenter assistants daily, inform supervisor of progress and problems.

VII. *Home Shows and Other Public Relations*
- Assist in constructing and manning home show booths, and other types of shows as requested.

VIII. *Job Estimating*
- Assist in estimating job materials and related costs as requested.

IX. *Continuing Education*
- Enroll in related courses, seminars, etc., working toward Certified Remodeler or other related accreditation.

HAMMERSMITH, INC.
Decatur, Georgia

Specializing in: . . . . .Design/Build, Upper-end Remodels
Number of Employees: . . . .18 (includes 7 lead carpenters)
Annual Sales Volume: . . . . .$2.9 million

JOB DESCRIPTION #4

Overall Responsibilities
The lead carpenter is completely responsible for the successful completion of the job, which includes being on time, on budget, and maintaining a high level of quality. In addition to being an excellent framing and finish carpenter, he or she should exhibit good judgment, high ethical standards, good oral and written communication skills, and strong leadership abilities.

Specific Duties
- Attend pass-the-baton meeting. Note all special considerations and priorities in job book.
- Maintain a clean, safe job site at all times. Ensure that the crew works in a safe manner, taking all reasonable precautions. Job site should be broom-swept at the end of day.
- Assign tasks to carpenters and helpers. Utilize carpenter and general labor, including yourself, in the most efficient and cost-effective manner.
- Coordinate all subcontractors in a knowledgeable manner. Be sure to give them ample lead time, and have the job ready for them to do their work.
- Anticipate ongoing needed materials, supplies, and drawings in advance.
- Deliver invoices to the office manager in a timely fashion.
- Order and monitor dumpster exchanges and final pickup. Keep track of shared dumpster costs with other job sites. Recycle as much as economically possible.
- Develop change orders in a timely fashion. Review with the production manager prior to submittal to the client. Change orders over $250 will

be generated by the production manager with input from lead carpenter. All change orders should be submitted as soon as they are signed.

- Walk through job site with production manager and client before insulation and drywall are installed to make sure all rough-in has been completed and is properly placed. Compare to plans and contract specs as an additional verification. (Client must sign pre-drywall checklist.)
- Verify placement of all mechanicals (especially electrical boxes) in a meeting with the production manager, client, and architect.
- Call building department for all necessary inspections well in advance.
- As job or phase nears completion, create a punchlist with the production manager. Turn over any punchlist items left at the end of the job to the production manager. The goal is for a zero punchlist job—long punchlists rob our profits.
- Review job-cost summaries every two weeks with the production manager and at the end of the job.
- Obtain the Certificate of Occupancy at the end of the job.
- Leave the job neat and clean, removing all tools, garbage cans, and job-site sign.

JOB DESCRIPTION #5

SASS CONSTRUCTION, INC.
Excelsior, Minnesota
Specializing in: . . . . .Remodeling and Insurance Repair Work
Number of Employees: . .13, including 3 lead carpenters
Annual Sales Volume: . . .$1.2 million

Title: Lead Carpenter
Line Relationship: Reports directly to the production manager
Supervises: Field staff and subcontractors

Job Summary
The lead carpenter is responsible for the job-site supervision of Sass Construction, Inc. personnel for all projects as assigned by the project manager. The lead carpenter will ensure that construction plans are followed as drawn or written, that all work is completed within quality and time guidelines set forth by the production manager. The lead carpenter is responsible for ensuring that job sites are maintained in a safe and orderly condition and that all Sass Construction and/or industry recognized safety guidelines are followed. This person will maintain field records for all assigned projects, including receipts for materials and equipment delivered to the job site. This person refers all matters for dispute regarding the project to the production manager.

Attire. Appropriate construction attire is expected. Hard-soled shoes or boots are required. Long pants and shirts are required, except that the project manager may authorize wearing of short pants in appropriate weather.

Hours. Work days are 8 hours per day (40 hours per week) from 7:30 a.m. to 4:00 p.m. There is one 30-minute lunch break and two 15-minute rest periods provided daily.

Specific Duties

1) Attend all project meetings and become familiar with work plans for all assigned projects. Assist in development of project schedules as requested.

2) Hands-on performance of all project-related demolition, framing and finish carpentry, drywall, painting, and/or other project-related tasks as may be assigned by or agreed upon with production manager. Provide job-site supervision of in-house construction personnel working at all assigned projects. Ensure compliance with all safety standards and guidelines.

3) Monitor the work performed by subcontractors on a daily basis, to ensure compliance with Sass Construction, Inc. standards related to quality of work, quantity of work, safety, and job-site behavior. Report any failure to comply with standards to the production manager immediately.

4) On a daily basis, maintain personnel time records and job reports for each project, turning documentation into the production manager by 7:15 a.m. on Monday of each week.

5) Through careful planning and foresight, notify the production manager in advance of impending material and subcontracted service requirements, ensuring that all purchases are referenced to an SCI Purchase Order number. Take delivery of materials and equipment needed for assigned projects, checking bills of loading and delivery tickets against actual materials received. Sign necessary documentation and turn into the project manager daily.

6) Follow tool check-out procedures for all tools to be taken from building. Sign out tools on the Equipment Check-Out Board. All tools removed from the building remain the responsibility of the lead carpenter until checked back in. Ensure proper use and care of equipment by all personnel, including lubricating as required. Ensure utilization of proper safety attachments and/or clothing in use of tools by all personnel. Notify the production manager of any malfunctioning tools or equipment.

7) The lead carpenter shall be responsible for the advance scheduling of all necessary inspections in order to maintain the project schedule. Follow-up on inspections to confirm successful outcomes.

8) The lead carpenter will be responsible for notification of subcontractors with regards to the advancing or delaying of the project timeline.

9) Document problems brought to his attention by field staff, subcontractors, and/or owner. Review and report these problems promptly

to the production manager. Authorize minor field corrections if appropriate and if corrections/changes do not alter project scope or cost. If problems relate to changes the customer desires on the project, stop work on the project immediately and call the production manager to the work site immediately.

10) Represent Sass Construction, Inc. in dealings with the customer in a dignified and professional manner. Monitor the Job-Site Communication Book and maintain open lines of communication with clients to ensure customer satisfaction. ◢

Chapter 5

Hiring And Training

ONCE YOU HAVE DEFINED THE JOB DESCRIPTION OF YOUR LEAD CARPENTER, YOU ARE ready to find someone to fill the role. Because the lead carpenter is such an important part of the team, you should take the same care and consideration in hiring this person as you take in hiring a salesman, office manager, or estimator.

As you know, the tradition within the remodeling industry is to focus attention on hiring a salesman because of the obvious importance he plays in the success of the company. In addition to interviews, companies often use personality tests and a host of other steps in the hiring process to ensure finding the right person for the job. They may even conduct role playing to see how the applicant will react in real sales situations.

But when it comes to hiring a lead carpenter, we often put an ad in the paper, receive 50 calls, and hire by asking ourselves the question, "Whom do I like best?" However, this is foolish. The lead carpenter is as important to the bottom line as the salesman. I would go so far as to say the lead carpenter is as important to the company's long-term success as the contractor. And certainly, the lead carpenter is as important to the success of each job as the production manager.

An important fact to realize is this: There will never be anyone, anywhere who fits your needs exactly. It is a fact of life that no one will meet our expectations from the very start. It is true in marriage, and it is true in business. And because this is true, realize that the ideal person you defined in your job description in Chapter 4 is just that, an ideal. Instead of rejecting every less-than-perfect applicant you encounter, realize that you will need to train even the best candidate to get exactly what you want.

Your Plan of Action: The Job Description

The job description is discussed in Chapter 4, but I will mention again here the importance of defining what you want and expect from someone in the position of a lead carpenter. The position is handled differently across the country and from company to company. To start, make a list of everything you want the lead carpenter to do in your company. Then weed out of that list anything that (1) you really want to keep under your control, or (2) you think might simply bog down a lead carpenter and make him less efficient.

Write out this list with brief explanations of what every item means. It should be easy to read and understand at a sixth-grade level. It should be self explanatory. Only when this is done should you move to the next step. Do not try to hire a lead carpenter without a job description; it will guide the remainder of the process.

The Advertisement

For some of us, this is the scary part. But it's actually the same approach as that used in marketing, where you focus on the people you want to work for, in the locations you want to work in, and toward the people who want to do business with your kind of company. In the case of hiring a lead carpenter, you want to attract people who can fill your job description. That means you don't want to attract people who are carpenters but who don't want to be a lead carpenter. You don't want concrete form carpenters. You don't want carpenters who are looking to fill in between other jobs. Therefore, any advertising must be done to attract the kind of people who have the skills and motivation you're looking for (Figure 6).

Structure your advertising, in whatever form, to suit the job description. Look through the job description to see what common themes you find in the

for interview (802) 123-1234.

REMODELING/ LEAD CARPENTERS

Remodeling Designs, Inc. is a nationally recognized leader in the residential remodeling industry. We have an opening in our production department for a Lead Carpenter. The ideal candidate will have 3+ years of experience as a Lead Carpenter in remodeling kitchens, baths, basements, and room additions. Excellent craftsmanship, work ethic, communication skills with customers, and appearance are very important qualities. In return, as a company, we offer excellent wages, company-match retirement plan, paid vacation, paid holidays, year-end performance bonus, uniforms, year-round work, an opportunity to advance within the company, and an enjoyable work environment. We are a company that hires people for long-term employment, therefore, all applicants are subject to drug screening and background checks. You can fax your resume to 937-555-5555, e-mail us at jobs@xyzconstruction.com, or call 937-555-6666 for a phone interview.

LITIGATION ATTORNEY
Needed for metropolitan area,
experienced attorney to carry out

Figure 6. "We're very picky," says Mike Cordonnier, president of Remodeling Designs in Dayton, Ohio, who ran this ad in a local newspaper. The ad was successful; it brought a highly qualified lead carpenter into the company.

items. For instance, you might find that ordering materials, scheduling subs, and managing paperwork all require "organizational skills." You may find that meeting with clients, supervising other employees, and working with you the contractor all require "good people skills." And most likely, you will need someone who is a skilled carpenter.

After you have identified the key elements, analyze how to express them with your candidate in mind. If you say "Carpenter Wanted," you may receive 50 phone calls from a wide range of people. If you say "Project Manager Wanted," you will receive a different set of responses. And "Lead Carpenter Wanted" will encourage yet another set of people to respond. The exact wording of the ad will be determined by the skills and aptitude you're looking for and which terms the tradespeople in your area use to describe these skills.

A term like "Good People Skills" has different meanings for many of us, and it may indeed be too vague a term. Perhaps saying "able to work with different kinds of people" may be easier to understand. Or perhaps "able to manage people efficiently" will catch the attention of someone who wants that kind of position. The point is to tailor the advertisement to match what you want in the job description.

Where should you advertise? Again, every market will be different, but there are some basic strategies you can follow.

Networking With Friends

Start by networking with friends of people in the company, including yourself. At Hopkins & Porter, some of our best employees have been people who were in the trades, already working for other companies, and who were friends of someone in our company. Let your employees know what you are looking for and ask: Do you know anyone?

Networking Within the Trades

Next, turn to acquaintances in the trades. Ask your subs, formally or informally. It is amazing how many subs work with carpenters on other jobs who just aren't fitting in with that company and are looking for a change. There are tremendous networking opportunities in that arena.

Also, talk with your suppliers. Talk with other business owners you may know through your trade association. One of our current lead carpenters came to us because he was being laid off from his job. His boss called us to see if we could hire him because he wanted to help him find a job with another good company.

Classified Ads

Finally, a classified ad in the local newspaper may be necessary. We usually do this as a last resort, simply because it takes a lot more time and effort to weed out the applicants who aren't what you're looking for. But once in a while a great employee comes on board because he happened to be looking when we were looking and saw our ad in the paper.

Wherever you look for a lead carpenter, refer to the job description; it will help you get what you want.

SCREENING

After the word is out, you will likely receive many calls and resumes. Determine how you will screen out unqualified people so that you only need to interview those who meet the minimum requirements. One way is to request a resume rather than a phone call. For example, one time, when we advertised for a lead carpenter but used the term "project manager" in the ad, we received resumes from bridge builders and high-rise superintendents, or from carpenters. But because we had resumes, we were able to sort through them easily and see which applicants had residential remodeling experience without taking the time to talk to every applicant or having to "reject" people personally. Finally, you can leave the screening up to someone else in the office. Train them to ask a few key questions over the phone and fill in a form. You can call the applicant back later if you like what you see. The job description can help you decide what questions to ask.

INTERVIEWING

The interview process should be designed to get you the information you need. This may seem obvious, but you would be surprised at how many construction company owners and managers conduct vague interviews. They sit down with an applicant and start asking questions as they come to mind. No plan. No notes. No objective way of determining the fit of this individual to the company.

For this process to work, however, and for you to increase your chances of finding a good candidate, you must have a plan and a clear, stated objective for the interview. For instance, is the end goal of this interview to see if this person should be called back for a second interview? Is the goal to decide whether to hire or not? Is the goal to get performance information to measure this person against the other applicants? The goal will help determine the questions you should ask.

With your goal in mind, develop questions designed to discover what you need to know based on your job description. The technical questions are easy. "Tell me about a roof you recently framed." "Describe how you would go about laying out a foundation for an addition." As in any interview, ask open-ended questions, and avoid questions that can be answered "yes" or "no." One of the qualities that you want to evaluate is: Can this person express himself to a stranger? Take note of this because the ease, or lack of ease, with which your applicant relates with you the first time you meet will likely be repeated with a new building or remodeling client.

SAMPLE HIRING QUESTIONS

1. Describe the best boss you've ever had. What did you like about him or her?
2. Describe the worst boss you've ever had. What did you dislike about him or her?
3. What is your idea of a productive day? Describe how it would run.
4. Tell what you would do to motivate a fellow employee who had to dig a footer.
5. Describe a time when a client has made you so frustrated you wanted to just walk off a job.
6. List five things that irritate you on a job site.
7. List five things that please you on a job site.
8. What are your long-term goals in life?
9. What are your long-term goals for work?
10. What is the first thing you do each day when you arrive on a job site?
11. Given that you are heading a three-person crew, name three ways that you can get the crew to work more productively.
12. Explain how the lead carpenter can affect the budget of a remodeling job.
13. What four important safety issues must be addressed on a remodeling job?
14. If I offered you an incentive to work more efficiently, what would motivate you?
15. On a remodeling project, who is responsible for meeting the budget?

Figure 7. *A list of open-ended questions—related to the qualities and skills outlined in your job description—will help you learn what you need to know about the applicant and keep the interview on track.*

The more difficult questions you'll ask applicants are those that involve intangible qualities, such as people skills or management skills. This is where you can borrow interview techniques from other companies, or perhaps from other fields. Figure 7 shows some sample questions our company uses. You may even want to hire a professional to help you write a set of effective interview questions. You can use a personality test to generate some of these questions. The important thing is to have these questions and tests in place before the actual interview starts.

With the process and questions in hand, conduct the interview. Stick with your plan. And remember, once you ask a question, be quiet and listen carefully. One of the most common mistakes of novice interviewers is that they talk too much, tell the applicant all about the job and the company, but don't learn enough about the applicant. Active listening techniques, such as repeating or paraphrasing the last few words of an answer can be helpful.

The applicant will have questions. In fact, you may want to ask the applicants if they have any questions, since this can be a good way to find out what's important to them in a job. In any event, applicants' questions are good, but be sure you don't get side-tracked from your own goals.

Finally, take notes during or right after the interview, while your impressions are still fresh. After conducting several interviews, you'll appreciate having written notes to refer to in making your final decision.

Making The Choice

After all this, the choice must be made at some point. Choose the person that best fits the job description based on the interviews. Avoid the "personality contest." "Which one do I like best?" is the wrong question to be asking yourself. A better question is: "Which applicant fits the job description best?" In fact, it may be to your advantage to hire somebody who is different from you. That may give the company a broader perspective. You may have greater adaptability if you and your employees have diverse styles, opinions, and ways of looking at the world.

However, if no one fits the job description, do not make a hire. You are better off struggling a little longer in your current situation than to hire someone who "might fit in with a lot of work."

On that note, I would like to talk about "continuous interviewing." Your interviewing process should be continually open. This is particularly easy if yours is a big company that has a good reputation among the trades. What it means is this: Always be willing to take an application and do interviews for anyone who fits your system. People will see your signs and stop by the office looking for a job. Perhaps you don't have an opening now. Let them know that, but interview them and keep the file on hand. This may allow you to hire quickly when the time comes.

Legal Considerations

I will not try to go into all the legal problems you can encounter when hiring someone, nor how to avoid these problems because that's beyond the scope of this book. However, it is important that you check with a lawyer or get some good books that are applicable to your state in order to avoid asking questions, verbally or in writing (as in forms), that are illegal. For instance, it's illegal in many states to ask a person his age or marital status or questions about physical or psychological handicaps. Best find that out before you receive a complaint or get involved in a lawsuit.

Salary And Benefits

Compensation for any position should be viewed in terms of the value of the whole package. We sell value to our clients. We don't sell the lowest price. The same is true in compensation for employees. The best value will attract the best people. Each company can put together whatever package fits their needs, but here are some ideas to include.

A Decent Wage

There are two ways to compensate employees. One is the traditional hourly wage. Lead carpenters should be compensated according to what they bring to the company. A lead that takes a large part of the job on himself should be paid for that extra work.

The second way to compensate is by salary. This is not common but has some real advantages. The employee has income he can count on and the company can expect work that won't always necessarily stop at the end of the standard work day. Be aware, however, that federal labor laws govern who can be paid a salary and who must be paid hourly. In general, a person must do primarily managerial or professional work to qualify for a salaried position. If you're not clear on this, consult your lawyer.

Stable Work Hours

With the increase in age of the work force, more and more carpenters have families. What's more, their spouses are probably working and can give less time to domestic concerns, leaving a need for your carpenter to be more involved. By providing consistent work hours, your employees can plan a schedule that will fit with the family's needs. Not only must the hours be consistent, but they must be virtually guaranteed.

Retirement Plan

The age of the work force, as well as the number of carpenters not associated with a union, creates an opportunity for a real benefit here. This is a savings benefit that can be initiated by the owner of a company. By helping carpenters put a little money away at each pay period, you are providing for their future. This is a plus because it helps the employees and it builds loyalty. If you show them that you are committed to them for the long haul, the chances increase that they will stay around longer.

Health Insurance

Many young carpenters will not see this as a benefit, but those with children will understand the enormous cost of being sick. Many people I know have forgone an hourly raise to be covered by health insurance for their family. This is a benefit that is going to increase in value as health care costs rise. It is not uncommon for this to be an annual benefit worth more than $5,000.

BONUSES

A great way to increase compensation is to give incentive bonuses. These are designed to create an incentive to complete the project within the budget. These bonuses can take many forms and we will show several examples here. But the bottom line is that a bonus must be something that provides incentive to workers.

quote from the field

"Our top guys make close to $25 an hour, with a week or two vacation, six paid holidays, and a $1 per hour bonus plan that they can put into medical care or dental... We pay them well."

BILL BALDWIN
Co-Owner
Hartman Baldwin
Claremont, California

Labor Only

This system works as follows: You show the budget to the lead carpenter, who accepts that the job can be done for that labor budget. He takes the job from there and when it is finished, if the entire labor budget was not used, the carpenter gets either all or part of the unused portion. The idea behind this is that the lead has a lot of control over the labor budget so he can choose to use additional help or not to stay within that budget.

Profit Sharing

Another approach many companies are turning to is a whole-company bonus system. This essentially means that, over the course of a year, if the company makes a profit, everyone receives a bonus. This system is designed to help everyone pull together as a team since it recognizes that it is not just the lead who helps make the money but the office people and the helpers as well. This type of bonus can then be invested in a retirement account or distributed as cash. The drawback to this system is there is no instant reward for good performance on a specific job.

On Budget, On Time, Satisfied Client

Some companies base the bonus on three measurable benchmarks:

1) Does the finished cost match or beat the budget? This can be checked quickly against the job costs that are kept for the job.

2) Was the project finished when it was promised? This can be determined as well by simply checking when the job was promised and when the clients moved into their new space.

3) Was the client satisfied with the work? This can be checked by issuing a questionnaire at the end of the job.

When these three items are established, the bonus can be paid. The carpenter or crew will get all or a percentage of the bonus, depending on how they did on the three benchmarks. The whole bonus amount can be established as a percentage of the budget, say 1 percent. For instance, an addition budgeted at $50,000 would have a total bonus of $500.

TRAINING

Once you hire a good employee, the training must start. Whether a person starts as a helper or as a capable lead carpenter, he must be trained. The helper needs to learn all about your company and about working with a lead carpenter. The experienced lead needs to know about how your company operates and exactly what it expects of a lead carpenter.

As we stated before, every company is different and a contractor who assumes that a carpenter will fit right into the company without training will be in for a big surprise. Many times I have been on a job site wondering why a carpenter has said or done a particular thing. When I

LEAD CARPENTER TRAINING MANUAL

1. Scheduling
2. Communication
3. Job Costing
   a. reading the estimate
   b. reading the budget report
   c. calculating percentage of gross profit
4. Time Cards
5. Job Logs
6. Good Planning
7. Change Orders
8. Working with People
   a. Subcontractors
   b. Inspectors
   c. Clients/Homeowners
   d. Bosses
   e. Employees
9. Subcontractors vs. Our Labor
10. Budgeting
11. Materials Lists
12. Attitudes
    a. positive
    b. service
    c. teamwork
14. Safety
15. Mission Statement and Policies
16. Company Habits
    a. clean job site
    b. company uniform
    c. being on time
    d. 15-minute morning break
    e. 30-minute lunch
    f. participating in company meetings
    g. handing in paperwork on time
17. Job Completion

Figure 8. *To create an effective training program, first write down a list of procedural items your lead carpenters must know. This list, or manual, can then be used to generate topics for specific training sessions.*

stopped and analyzed the situation, I often found that the carpenter had never been told how we wanted it done.

A good example is the wrap-up of a job. We have developed a system for the lead carpenter to start wrapping up the job three weeks before we are actually finished. If we follow this procedure, we end up with fewer punchlist items and more satisfied clients. However, because this runs counter to the norm, which is to simply announce that the job is

Train for success. *Lead carpenters—and other employees as well—need to be trained in how your company does things. Remember, carpenters are not mind-readers.*

over and that it's time for the punchlist, we have to train our lead carpenters differently. But with a little training, we are able to get them to focus on the end of the job before they are actually finished.

Plan For Training

Good training, like other important business strategies, requires good planning. Any training program must be written down and systematized. The first thing to do is to make a list of all the items that you want your lead carpenters (or entire field staff) to know. This will be an extensive list. In general, I am not talking about technical skills. These will be learned on the job and are, to a large extent, the same in all companies. What I am talking about are the procedural items that they must know to work in this company. Figure 8 gives a list that you can start with.

Training Agenda

With this list of procedural items in hand, start grouping similar ideas into topics that can be taught or discussed in about an hour. You will find that the list becomes significantly smaller in this process. You now have segments for your training. Each segment should be a self-contained unit so that each person who attends gets the whole package each time. Use a similar format each time so that it becomes a regular pattern. This will help the employees know what to expect. Here is a sample of the training agenda used at Hopkins and Porter:

Training Segment #1: Mission Statement and Policies
Training Segment #2: Company Habits
Training Segment #3: Attitudes
Training Segment #4: Job Costing
Training Segment #5: Proper Job Planning
Training Segment #6: Scheduling
Training Segment #7: Safety
Training Segment #8: Change Orders
Training Segment #9: Final Completion of a Job
Training Segment #10: Working with Inspectors
Training Segment #11: People Skills
Training Segment #12: Managing Employees

Training Segment #13: Working with Subcontractors
Training Segment #14: Material Management
Training Segment #15: Job Logs
Training Segment #16: Time Cards

Beyond this, the training segments need to be broken down into their component parts. This outline helps the trainer prepare and present the training clearly and concisely. All the segments and the material needed for them should be well organized in a binder so that when the time for training comes around, the material is readily available.

A Sample Training Session

As an example, here is Segment #12 from Hopkins and Porter's training program, broken out in outline form:

TRAINING SEGMENT #12

Topic: Managing Employees
Trainer(s): Tim Faller and Mike Denker
Preparation: Put out topic in Hopkins/RePorter (our weekly, in-house newsletter)
Materials Needed by Trainer: Role-play scenarios
Content:
• The importance of the one-man crew
• What are the lead carpenters' responsibilities on the site?
• Hiring and firing responsibilities
• How can the lead maximize efficiency on site?
• Lists
• Meetings
• Disciplined breaks
• Dividing job into mini jobs
• Goal setting on a job site

Follow-up Exercise: None
Timetable: 1 hour
Actual Time:
Date of Training:
Trainer's Notes:

When and Where To Train

In deciding when and how to train employees, there are two considerations: the immediate needs and the long-term needs. When you notice that an employee has a particular issue which needs immediate attention, that is the time to address it. Do not wait. This comes up when an indi-

"The lead carpenter has to be... part psychologist, part philosopher... and ace carpenter. Teaching someone to be an ace carpenter is easy. Teaching someone to be good with people is not easy."

BILL BALDWIN
Co-Owner
Hartman Baldwin
Claremont, California

vidual is hired and as he goes about his work. Some employees need to be trained on a number of topics from the first day they start with the company. Good examples are Segment #2 on "Company Habits" and Segment #16 on filling in a "Time Card."

Others can be used along the way for training as needed. For example, if you note that a particular lead is having trouble with subcontractors, you can bring out Segment #13 and go over it either right on the site or back in the office.

The other method for training is to cover all the segments sequentially at regular intervals. Spaced repetition is a valuable tool for getting the message across. Our company does training at company meetings once a month for all field staff together, including lead carpenters. The field staff comes to the office on company time. The company provides some drinks and pizza and we do training and discuss issues of current interest to the company.

What we have found, however, is that unless we use the agenda in the outline above, we cover the same issues over and over— the nuisance items that are bugging us the most that week. *With* the agenda, the meetings are far more productive. We address all of the company needs over the space of 16 months.◪

Chapter 6

The Production Manager's Role

IS A PRODUCTION MANAGER REALLY NECESSARY?

*AS I TRAVEL AROUND THE COUNTRY TEACHING SEMINARS ABOUT THE LEAD CARPEN-*ter system, I am often asked this question: If the lead carpenter does all of this work, what does the production manager do? The sassy answer is "drink coffee and collect a paycheck." The correct answer is what we will cover in this chapter.

As we have discussed already, the lead carpenter system is an ideal. And if a company can implement and use it flawlessly, it may never need a production manager. But there are two realities that can make a production manager a necessity.

First is the fact that no one will implement this system perfectly. That's because there are people involved with various skills, aptitudes, and personalities. You will find that there are certain parts of the job that a given lead carpenter will not be able to handle. Related to this is the fact that all lead carpenters grow into the system gradually. None performs perfectly in the job the day he is hired. Whether it is technical skills or managerial skills, no one has it all. This is where the production manager comes in. He is the person who fills in the missing pieces for each of the lead carpenters.

In our company, a particular lead carpenter has trouble dealing with homeowners. Sometimes, he's just not good with people. Of course, we could fire him and hire someone else. But the new person would come to us with some other deficiency — perhaps an inability to motivate others. Instead, we keep our otherwise splendid lead carpenter and allow the production manager to be more involved with the client relations on these particular jobs. Another lead carpenter in our company has trouble scheduling subs. He just hasn't gotten the knack of it yet. In this case, the

"The lead carpenter is responsible for a successful job, but the production manager plays a supportive role: for instance, he walks through with the client and the lead before the drywall goes on, and at the end of the job, they both make up the punchlist."

WRIGHT MARSHALL
Production Manager
HammerSmith, Inc.
Decatur, Georgia

production manager pays more careful attention to the sequence of the job in order to ensure good scheduling.

The second reality that calls for a production manager is related to the first—growth. If a company remains relatively small, say under $750,000 in volume, any inadequacies of the lead carpenters can be picked up by the salesperson or contractor. Above a certain volume, however, a company will need an additional level of management to ensure a high-quality product and service. The dollar volume where this becomes necessary depends on both the training of the lead carpenters and the number of jobs that make up the volume.

For instance, if a company does two jobs a year but they are worth $500,000 each, two leads and the contractor can probably handle the work without any problem. The contractor is able to focus attention on the project, not on selling the next job. And with only two leads, it's easy for the contractor to relate to each and to effectively pass information along.

However, if a company is doing 20 jobs of $50,000 each, we're looking at a totally different story. In this case, the contractor is busy trying to sell another job because several current jobs will end soon and his people will need a place to go. Plus, there are probably five different leads with disparate personalities who need support. And at any given time there are perhaps 10 different homeowners who are calling for someone's attention. This is where a production manager becomes important.

QUALIFICATIONS REQUIRED

As I've discussed earlier in the book, lead carpenters must have—or be willing and able to learn—a wide range of skills. The same is true of production managers. I would separate these skills into two areas: (1) knowledge of technical skills, and (2) ability to inspire others.

Technical Expertise

It is important for the production manager to have good knowledge of the technical skills required for all phases of construction. However, it's not necessary for him to be proficient in all phases of construction. Many of the carpenters who have worked for me are more proficient at cutting a miter or working out a rafter detail than me, a production manager. For example, one lead carpenter I work with can precut a hip roof on the ground, then assemble it. And it works. If I was doing the job, I would have to cut and fit each piece. But I do understand how the whole project goes together. I understand the mechanics of construction and have a working knowledge of all the trades involved.

This knowledge is important for many reasons. The first is eliciting respect from carpenters, who will have trouble listening to and respecting a supervisor who doesn't know construction. But aside from that, this knowledge is important because of quality control. Here are a few scenarios to illustrate my point. Several years ago, the electrical codes changed in our area so that more outlets were required in a kitchen. However, the electrician had not been brought up to speed, nor had the lead carpenter. It happens that I had encountered the problem on another job and mentioned it to the electrician. We were able to rectify the problem before the inspector held up the job.

Here's another scenario to consider: Have you ever had a situation where a carpenter had it in his mind that a framing detail could only be done a certain way? This can be a particular problem when a carpenter is hired from another part of the country. He is going to do things his way by default. When this happens, a good knowledge of the technical data will allow the production manager to step in and make cost-effective decisions.

A corollary to this qualification is a desire to learn new ways of building. Changes in materials and techniques are all around us. Added to that, homeowners are more and more educated about different methods of construction. They are keeping up with air infiltration standards, for instance, as well as efficiency ratings, insulation values, and special products. They are reading the trade magazines and seeing ideas that catch their imagination. They want their contractors to be aware of those things as well.

Aside from our clients wanting new and better materials and techniques, the building codes are changing all around us. Two recent situations come to mind. In the first instance, we weren't aware of a new rule that required us to leave the energy rating stickers on our windows until after the close-in inspection. On one job, an efficient carpenter had them all removed. When the job was inspected, we found out about the new code and the production manager quickly put out a memo to everyone else in the company to avoid this problem.

A second situation happened when a non-tempered window was ordered for a location too close to the floor (in our area the minimum is 18 inches). This was not the lead carpenter's fault, nor could we expect him to find the solution on his own. As the production manager, though, I contacted the inspectors and found out what was permissible with respect to a solution. I then contacted the company that was certified to install the special film that would make the window safe, and thereby rectified the problem.

Ability To Inspire Others

A production manager must be able to inspire others and motivate them to work efficiently. This is a labor-intensive business, and to be competitive a company must be efficient. This relates closely to a company's profits and, therefore, its future and viability. The production manager plays

Safety First. *In some companies, the production manager leads safety meetings and fulfills OSHA requirements. Here, a production manager shows employees how to properly use a safety harness.*

a significant role in emphasizing and promoting efficient labor. This means keeping an eye out for inefficient methods, and finding ways to improve them.

Below are listed other related qualities a production manager needs to have to be effective:

Ability to train others. Because the production manager interacts with the field staff on a regular basis, he is involved in the company's training process. He could play only a minor role in the training process, but at times he'll be the best person to train personnel directly on particular subjects.

Good communication skills. Much of the production manager's job is passing along or discussing information. It is imperative that he communicates well with peers, clients, and bosses. He needs to be able to listen carefully to people and be able to show that he cares about another's concerns. He needs to be able to speak in ways that others can understand. The ability to speak on several levels is important because of the broad range of people with whom he will interact.

Concern for the details of the project. The production manager will likely give the final check on the quality of the project. He will be working with the field staff to make the project work from the "bottom up." His concern for details must match the contractor's to ensure a consistent product.

Ability to follow through. Related to the previous topic is the need to be able to follow through on the little details that seem to plague each project. Inevitably, there are items that just can't be decided or resolved before the lead carpenter must move on to another project. Some of these require a great deal of tenacity to complete. Sometimes satisfying a client and collecting the final check is a task that requires the hanging-on capacity of a bulldog. Although this follow-through can be done by the lead carpenter, this task often falls to the production manager after the lead has moved to another job. This is particularly true if the clients start using the space before the final check is paid and they begin to find "defects."

Can Leads Become Production Managers?

Once the qualities are spelled out, a natural question is: Can a lead carpenter become a production manager? The company I work for certainly thinks so! They have promoted two leads to this position. Here's what I have found over the years from talking with people about promoting leads to production managers.

First of all, a lead carpenter needs to understand that the satisfaction of building a job from start to finish is not a part of the production manager's role. This can be a big jolt to people who derive satisfaction and self-esteem from their creative abilities.

Second, the lead carpenter may feel like this is a step up and be disappointed that it is simply a change of responsibility. Lead carpenters should feel like they are valuable and a part of the team. Teamwork implies that everyone plays a part and no part is of greater value in the process. It may also mean there is no increase in pay or benefits.

Here's a third point to consider: Is a particular lead carpenter suited to the job of production manager? The ability to produce a job does not necessarily mean an ability to coach or manage others in producing a job. It's true that it's impossible to help others do their job without having some personal knowledge of their work. But the ability to help others is not automatic. If a lead carpenter has demonstrated an ability to work with people, manage subs, and handle paperwork (the management stuff) for individual jobs, he will probably make a good production manager. And another good test: Is he well organized? With as many as 10 jobs to oversee, the production manager starts juggling many aspects of a job and must be organized, or there will be chaos.

And fourth, do you really want to take a good carpenter out of the field and try to retrain him? This is a serious question. These really are different types of jobs and a good lead carpenter is hard to find. It may be easier to bring in people with good managerial skills and train them to be production managers, and use your best carpenters in the field as leads.

THE JOB DESCRIPTION

The following list is an example of a job description you might hand to your production manager. You can also use it as an aid in the hiring process. (Figure 9 shows how another company defines its production manager job description.)

Supervise all lead carpenters in their daily work, providing technical help as needed, support working with the client, training for leads on supervision of the job, and motivation for more efficient production.

The key role for a production manager is to supervise. It is his job to oversee the big picture, not to be entangled in the minutia of the project. He must see the big picture. Supervision essentially means to provide support for the lead carpenters, which includes a wide variety of tasks. Sometimes it means showing them a better way to do a job. Sometimes

PRODUCTION MANAGER JOB DESCRIPTION

■ **PRE-CONTRACT**

• Assist in estimating. Meet subcontractors at jobs for estimates and special material pricing.

• Give input regarding budget, time requirements, scope of work, personnel qualifications, selection of lead carpenter, adequacy of plans and drawings, and stock and custom materials.

■ **PRE-PRODUCTION**

• Create schedules.

• Provide lead carpenter with all necessary information and special order materials to start job. This information includes a schedule, scope of work, budget, and special material lists.

• Line up initial subcontractors to allow lead carpenter to hit the ground running. Order long lead time items (e.g., windows).

• Create subcontractor contracts detailing each trade's scope of work.

• Conduct pass-the-baton meeting with lead carpenter, architect, and homeowners.

■ **PRODUCTION**

• Visit job sites weekly to review progress; anticipate complications; monitor safety, security, job-site appearance; gauge client's satisfaction; and check job-site appearance.

• Act as a resource for leads by following through on questions, pursuing difficult information, rescheduling subcontractors and materials, making scheduling changes, troubleshooting, and reassuring clients.

• Coordinate invoices and progress payments. Verify that change orders are kept up to date and priced correctly. Review change orders to see if company is earning required margin.

• Attend pre-drywall walkthrough with lead and client. Have lead sign pre-drywall checklist. Have client sign change waiver.

• Monitor invoice coding. Monitor subcontractor contract compliance.

• As job nears completion, make sure homeowner compiles punchlist. Complete job completion form. Follow up on punchlist.

• Ensure that job receives required inspections and Certificate of Occupancy.

■ **POST-PRODUCTION**

• Follow up with client concerns and questions.

• Post job reviews to determine profit margin, job-cost coding, schedule issues, design problems, and other issues. Check that all invoices have been coded correctly. Give estimating feedback.

■ **GENERAL**

• Install, clean, take down, and stock job-site signs. Assist contractor in hiring and evaluating all production staff.

• Make production reports at weekly meetings, review job status, job costs, and other relevant issues.

• Review job cost and schedules with homeowners on a weekly basis.

• Lead monthly safety meetings and fulfill Hazcom/OSHA requirements.

• Compile, coordinate, and schedule all warranty work.

• Coordinate laborers and carpenters.

• Research new subcontractors and suppliers.

• Keep up to date on material pricing and new products.

• Maintain associate list.

■ **OTHER**

• Possible small job supervision.

• Convert format for estimating and job cost.

Figure 9. *This job description from HammerSmith, Inc., of Decatur, Ga., shows how the production manager acts as a key support person to the lead carpenters.*

it means tracking down a sub during the day to find out a critical piece of information. Sometimes it means challenging the lead to use his time better and increase production. Sometimes it means placing an order for the lead. Sometimes it even means providing a little manual labor when the helper didn't show up.

***Run and participate in periodic site meetings with the home-
owners of each job*** to discuss progress, problems, and changes.
Although the lead carpenter will have regular interaction with the homeowner, the production manager will want to "take the client's temperature." In many situations, the lead carpenter and homeowner develop a
relationship that makes it difficult for the homeowner to complain or
point out problems to the lead. The invitation to do this, extended by the
production manager as a third party, can help to bring out many hidden
fears or problems. In some cases, the production manager also becomes
the official management representative.

***Be the conduit of information from the office to the field, and
be a good decision-maker.*** One of the biggest problems with growth
in any company is the smooth flow of information. Miscommunicated
information can cause costly and sometimes irreparable mistakes. The
production manager becomes the conduit for all information from the
office to the lead carpenter.

Why is this important? If there is only the homeowner, the lead carpenter, and the contractor/salesperson, the job is easy. If the lead carpenter has a question, he simply asks the contractor. As the company grows,
the contractor/salesperson become less available when needed, and typically he begins to leave details out of the specs and plans. The carpenter
needs the information and begins calling to ask anyone who will give him
an answer. The homeowner may give one answer, the architect another,
and the office manager another. The production manager is the person
who can resolve this. To do so, he must be familiar enough with the plans
and specs to understand the intent of the project.

***Review potential jobs with the salesman to ensure proper bud-
geting and specification.*** The lead carpenter system depends on accurate information being passed to the carpenters. It would be nice if the
carpenters had the time to review every contract and spec for accuracy.
But they do not. This is especially true of overall job budgets. As a job
lead progresses through the process of sales, it is important that someone
from the production side of the company reviews the job. This will help
catch errors, identify problem areas, and clarify how the job will be carried out before promises are made to the homeowners. Because of his
knowledge of production, the production manager can help produce a
better sale for the company.

Act as a liaison between the field and the sales staff. One of the
major problems in construction is in relations between labor and management. It doesn't matter how hard you work at it, it seems there is
inherent distrust between the two. If production managers have field
experience, they can help bridge this gap by helping each side understand how the other thinks.

***Schedule the sequence of jobs, who will work on the job, and
who will help.*** As the company grows, it will be important to have a
clearinghouse for resources that are needed by the lead carpenters. This

can be done by the production manager. Each lead carpenter is responsible for using the right resources to bring his job in on budget. But in a larger company, this sometimes puts him in conflict with the needs of other lead carpenters.

For example, every company has some helpers who are better than others. Suppose two lead carpenters want the same helper at the same time. Somebody has to decide who does what. The same thing happens with subcontractors. Two leads are reaching the same point in their schedule at the same time. (Isn't it amazing how many times jobs finish at the same time regardless of when they start?) Your company uses a particular sub a lot and he is assigned to those two jobs. Who gets the sub on what day? Somebody has to decide.

Work on the computer to track, review, and monitor job costs. It is important to continuously review the status of costs on each job. In small companies this can be done by the contractor. As the company grows, however, this can become impossible. The production manager can absorb this responsibility and review the progress of each job on a regular basis, helping to make adjustments as the job progresses.

Regularly evaluate and review field staff. Part of managing is evaluating people, assessing their strengths and weaknesses. This should be done by someone who observes an employee's everyday behavior and performance. In larger companies, it is not possible for the contractor the company to personally evaluate each employee. The production manager can do this because of his more informed knowledge of each person's work. ◢

Chapter 7

Profit and the Lead Carpenter

TO UNDERSTAND THE RELATIONSHIP BETWEEN PROFIT AND THE LEAD CARPENTER, WE must first step back and establish the purpose of any remodeling project. This can be looked at from several points of view. The client may want more space and an undefined level of "quality." The carpenter may look at it from an artistic perspective and see a chance to show off his craftsmanship. But we must look at it primarily from the viewpoint of the contractor.

The contractor, as the owner of the company, views the project primarily as a source of income. Not only is it income for the company, but it is the owner's bread and butter. Many companies are small and need to make a profit on each job to survive.

To fit into this reality, the lead carpenter may need to change his mindset about what motivates him to complete each project. Whatever reasons the lead carpenter has for going to work, all must be tempered and shaped by the understanding that he is on the job to make money for the company. I will spend the next few pages discussing how that happens. (It is crucial that the lead carpenter understands how the company makes, and can lose, money; therefore I've included sample problems for practice at the end of the chapter.)

FISCAL MANAGEMENT BASICS

Many people believe that the finances of a business are handled in the same manner that most of us handle our personal checkbooks: The contractor receives payments from a client, makes deposits into the company account, and then pays bills, payroll, and taxes. When the money runs out he scurries around to find more by collecting payments or by borrowing. With this type of accounting the company lives week to week, never really knowing where it stands or if it will survive the year.

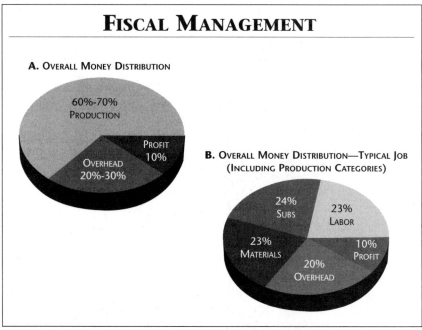

FISCAL MANAGEMENT

A. OVERALL MONEY DISTRIBUTION

60%-70%
PRODUCTION

PROFIT
10%

OVERHEAD
20%-30%

B. OVERALL MONEY DISTRIBUTION—TYPICAL JOB
(INCLUDING PRODUCTION CATEGORIES)

24%
SUBS

23%
LABOR

23%
MATERIALS

10%
PROFIT

20%
OVERHEAD

Figure 10. All money in the company goes to either production, overhead, or profit. Production costs are further broken down into materials, subs, and labor. These areas are where the lead carpenter has the greatest influence.

The reality is that a good contractor projects, into the year ahead, the sales of the company, the production costs of the company, and the estimated profit. Each of these is based on available personnel, sales experience, and good judgment. This projection provides a plan for the growth of the company and includes net profit after all production costs and overhead costs have been covered.

So how does a company make a profit on its product? The answer in its simplest form is "sell high and produce low," thereby creating a surplus of money at the end. In other words, when all of the bills have been paid that are associated with that project, and all of the contract money has been collected, there is more money taken in than there is spent.

There are three main areas of fiscal management for any company: overhead, production, and profit. Depending on the company profile, the percentages will vary but they could look like the following: profit at 10%, production at 60% to 70%, and overhead at 20% to 30% (Figure 10A).

THE BIG BLEND: OVERHEAD, PRODUCTION, AND PROFIT

A company's overhead is usually figured as a lump sum each year, and if no significant changes are made, it can remain pretty constant for many

STANDARD FORMULAS FOR FIGURING NET PROFIT

Sales Price ($) – Production Costs ($) = Gross Profit
($125,000)   –   ($87,500)   = ($37,500)

Sales Price ($) ÷ Gross Profit ($) = Gross Profit Percentage (%)
($125,000) ÷   ($37,500)   =   (33%)

Sales Price ($) x Overhead (%) = Overhead ($)
($125,000)   x   (20%)   = ($25,000)

Gross Profit ($) x Overhead (%) = Overhead ($)
($125,000)   x   (20%)   = ($25,000)

Gross Profit ($) – Overhead ($) = **Net Profit ($)**
($37,500)   – ($25,000)   = **($12,500)**

Figure 11. Net profit, the money left after all production costs and overhead costs are covered, is necessary for a company to survive. An increase in overhead or production costs means a decrease in profits.

years. However, production costs—which are generally broken down into the three categories of materials, labor, and subcontractors—can vary greatly from job to job. But in the typical remodeling company, each of these three main categories amounts to about one-third of total production costs. The exact percentages will depend, of course, on how much work is done in-house and how much is subcontracted, the value of fixtures and finish materials and who supplies them, as well as many other factors. What is important is for the lead carpenter to understand the percentages of the company that he works for and the percentages allocated for each job.

If you look at Figure 10B, you can see the overall distribution of all moneys associated with a typical job (including the breakdown of production costs). We can see that we still have the projected 10% profit, 20% overhead, 23% labor, 23% materials, and 24% subcontractors. These numbers are critical if we are to understand how much money the lead carpenter has control over.

For example, let's suppose we have a job that sells for $125,000. Profit has been projected at 10% ($12,500), and overhead is allocated to the job at 20% ($25,000). Production costs would be as follows: 23% for labor ($28,750); 23% for materials ($28,750); and 24% for subcontractors ($30,000). That means on this job the lead carpenter would be directly responsible for production costs totaling $87,500.

Some standard formulas for figuring these percentages are shown in Figure 11.

Overhead

Overhead is generally defined as the cost of managing the business itself. This includes items like rent on an office, computer systems, phone bills, pagers, insurance for the company, salaries of office staff and principals in the company (assuming they do not swing a hammer), and the cost of training and company parties.

The contractor, not the lead carpenter, controls most overhead costs. One exception is worker's compensation insurance. Although this is an overhead item, it can be influenced by the lead carpenter through his role in trying to control the number and severity of accidents on the job. But, for the most part, overhead costs are out of the lead carpenter's hands.

Production

By contrast, production costs are directly under the control of the lead carpenter. Production costs are everything associated with the cost of producing the product, including employee wages, tool rentals, material costs, subcontractor costs, insurance for production workers, labor taxes, and utilities fees.

The lead carpenter controls material costs by making wise decisions about the type, quantity, and waste factors of the materials on the site. Labor costs come under his control because he is responsible for managing other carpenters and their production output. Lead carpenters even have control over subcontractor costs by limiting extras and overruns on the site.

So for the lead carpenter, the focus should be on production costs. Consider the job of $125,000 with production costs estimated at $87,500. This is money that the lead carpenter has control over. This is a lot of money for the contractor, in essence, to hand over to a carpenter with the words, "Please build this project at this price."

Profit

All of these factors—overhead, production costs, sales price, and profit — are locked together in a balance. It is obvious that, when the selling price is fixed, profits decrease as costs increase. But the other relationships are less obvious.

Let's look at how these factors are related:

Overhead vs. volume. The volume of sales is the sales price of all jobs sold by a company in a given time frame, typically a year. The volume affects overhead in that as the volume of sales increases, the overhead percentage generally decreases. That's because many overhead costs stay the same. If you could double the volume and keep real overhead costs constant, it would look like this:

- If Volume of sales is: $500,000
  Overhead costs are: . . . .$100,000 (or 20%)

- If Volume of sales increases to: $1,000,000
  Overhead stays at: . . . .$100,000 (or 10%)

In reality, some overhead costs, like worker's comp, go up with volume if you have more employees. But in many instances, increasing the volume can lower your overhead percentage.

Profit vs. production costs. Profit is a function of production costs if volume and overhead remain constant, as shown below:
- If Volume of sales is $500,000
  Overhead is 20% $100,000

- If Production costs are 70% $350,000
  Then Profit is 10% . . . .$ 50,000

- If Volume of sales remains at $500,000
  And if Overhead remains at 20% $100,000
  Production costs decrease to 60% $300,000
  Then Profit increases to 20% $100,000

HOW TO INCREASE PROFITABILITY

Lower Overhead

Lowering operating costs is one way to increase profits. Overhead can grow without good reason and should always be checked to see what a company really needs to spend. For example, a company may have an assistant in the office who orders materials and schedules subcontractors. If these responsibilities are given to the lead carpenters then there may be room to cut that job and reduce overhead. In general, it is the responsibility of the owner of the company to keep the overhead as low as possible.

The lead carpenter can contribute to the lowering of overhead by maintaining a safe work area. Worker's compensation costs are a large part of any company's insurance bill and are directly affected by the work on a site. A simple accident can cause rates to rise from 10% to 30% of the payroll very quickly and have a big impact on profitability. The lead carpenter, by keeping a safe record, can help keep the rate very low.

Sell the Job Higher

The most obvious way to increase profit is to increase the sales price of the job. Salespeople always try to sell a job as high as they can, but there are limits to how much a remodeling project is worth to any given client. The way in which a lead carpenter can affect this end of the business is small but needs to be mentioned. By keeping good records and maintaining a good relationship with the sales staff, a lead carpenter can and should affect the way in which estimates are done. By getting real feedback from lead carpenters, the estimators can be more accurate on the next estimate, and sell the job at a better profit.

Control Production Costs

The responsibility for this, of course, falls upon the lead carpenter. Production costs are made up of labor, subs, and materials, so any savings must come from these areas. We will mention them here for reference only, and will provide more detail later in the book.

There are essentially three ways to lower labor costs on the job: we can lower wages, reduce manpower, or increase productivity—or some combination of these. I haven't met a worker yet who was in favor of lowering wages, including myself. At times this may be necessary, but in general the alternatives are more acceptable.

Fortunately, there are several ways to reduce manpower. You can use smaller crews (this will be addressed in detail in Chapter 9). Or you can use lower-paid people to do the job. If a helper will suffice, use a helper. If a laborer will work, use a laborer. If a temporary laborer will fit the bill, use a temp. We make a mistake when we think in terms of whom we like to work with instead of who will be most profitable for the job. Vary the crew to meet the needs of that particular task or phase of the job.

But the bottom line is that the lead carpenter must start thinking in terms of using assistance only when required. If a helper is needed to set the rafters and nail down decking, for example, he should be sent to another job as soon as those tasks are complete. If extra people are kept on the job, it will end up costing money instead of saving money.

Finally, you can strive for more production per worker. This is the process of doing more with what you have. Most people, if they have achieved the level of skill needed to be a carpenter, pride themselves on their work. They are likely to feel insulted if anyone thinks that they can work faster or better. However, there are ways the lead carpenter can encourage more productivity from himself and from crews:

- Use a weekly schedule to set goals. As the saying goes: "If you aim at nothing, you will hit it."
- Plan each day carefully. If the day runs itself, there will be chaos and money lost. Make lists of the work that has to be done that day. This allows everyone on the job to know what must be accomplished without waiting to be told. The lead carpenter cannot assume that other workers will know automatically what has to be done when.
- Take fewer breaks. Breaks are a good idea for safety and morale, but can become big money losers if not watched carefully. A few extra minutes added on the end of each break over a six-month job will increase the labor budget considerably.
- Initiate good clean-up habits. A clean work site will increase productivity. Organize your space. The less time you spend trying to figure out "where you put it," the more productive you will be.
- Try a four-day week. If your company allows it, scheduling four 10-hour days per week means less set up and cleanup per hour of production.
- Provide incentive programs. If the lead is given the authority to do this, he can provide incentives like, "If we get this done by 2:30, everyone can go home early."

LABOR BURDEN WORKSHEET

Hourly wage . . . .$	15.00

Federal PR Taxes:

FICA @ 6.2% . . . .$	.93
Medi @ 1.45% . . . .$	.22
FUTA @ .008% . . . .$	.01

State PR Taxes:

SUI/ETT @ 5.4%* . . . .$	.81

Other Payroll Expenses:

Workers' Compensation @ 15% . . . .$	2.25
General Liability @ 2% . . . .$	.30
Vacation/Holiday @ 4% . . . .$	.60
Medical/Life Insurance @ 10% . . . .$	1.50
Retirement/401(k) @ 3% . . . .$	.45

Other @_____% . . . .$	
Total Cost of Employee Labor . . . .$	22.07

*Check with either the IRS or your accountant for gross wage ceilings on these amounts.

Figure 12. The importance of staying within a job's labor budget is made clear by understanding the real cost or "labor burden" of each employee working there.

In thinking about productivity it is important to realize that a carpenter's hourly pay does not represent what that person costs the company to employ. Due to the labor "burden" from worker's comp, federal and state taxes, vacation and sick time, and any other benefits, real costs are at least 33% higher, and often greater than that (Figure 12).

If the "burden" on wages is 33%, then a $15 per hour wage is really $20 per hour. The exact rates will vary from state to state but the lead carpenter should be aware of what they are for his company. Regardless of the exact rate of labor burden, labor is typically the largest expense under the direct control of the lead carpenter. Since labor overruns can have a big impact on the profitability of a job, it is imperative that a lead carpenter understand a job's labor budget and do everything possible to stay within it.

Cut costs of materials. Another way to cut production dollars and increase profit is to reduce materials costs. In general, the materials for a job are going to cost what they cost, but by learning a few simple tricks you can save time and money in small ways that will add up over the months to real savings. For example, make a material list early, check deliveries carefully, shop materials regularly, return unusable material immediately, always have materials delivered, and cover all materials stored outside as soon as they are delivered.

Control subs. By working closely with the subs, the third area of production costs can be controlled. By being on the site and by planning ahead, a lead carpenter can avert extra charges, reworks, and delays in the

SAMPLE PROBLEMS FOR LEAD CARPENTERS

PROBLEM A

The company you work for needs an addition built on a house. The dimensions are 12x14 feet, with the 14-foot dimension projecting from the house. The labor budget to frame the addition is $1,625. Your resources are as follows:

> If you work by yourself $20/hr
> If you work with an experienced helper $35/hr
> If you work with a laborer $30/hr

You have figured that it will take you, by yourself, two days to frame the floor system. Another two days, by yourself, to frame and sheathe the walls. For the roof, you believe you need help so you figure in an experienced helper for four days. You work an 8-hour day. You plan to take a 15-minute break each day in the morning. The company allows you to set up your tools "on the clock." That usually takes 15 minutes.

- How much will the labor cost to frame this addition?   *$1,760*

- Are you over or under the budget?   *Over*

- If you are over budget, how can you change your work plan to meet your budget?

  Use a laborer instead of a helper. At four days to frame the roof, you would save $160. Total labor cost would be $1,600 and would keep you under budget.

PROBLEM B

The overall production budget for the project is $18,325. The sales price is $28,936. The company overhead percentage is 28%.

- What is the gross profit?

  Sales price-production cost = gross profit
  *$28,936 – $18,325 = **$10,611***

- What is the gross profit percentage?

  Gross profit – sales price = gross profit percentage
  *$10,611÷ $28,936 = **37%***

- What is the overhead (in dollars)?

  Sales price x overhead percentage = overhead (dollars)
  *$28,936 x .28 = **$8,102***

- What is the net profit?

  Gross profit ÷ overhead = net profit
  *$10,611 – $8,102 = **$2,509***

- What is the net profit percentage?

  Net profit ÷ sales price = net profit percentage
  *$2,509 ÷ $28,936 = **8.7%***

If you exceed your cost budget by $1,275:

- What is your new gross profit?   *$28,936 – $18,325 – $1,275 = **$9,336***

- What is your new gross profit percentage?

  New gross profit ÷ sales price = new gross profit percentage
  *$9,336 ÷ $28,936 = **32%***

- What is your new net profit?

  New gross profit – overhead (dollars) = new net profit
  *$9,336 – $8,102 = **$1,234***

- What is your new net profit percentage?

  New gross profit ÷ sales price = new net profit percentage
  *$1,234 ÷ $28,936 = **4.3%***

job—all of this saving the company time and money. I will talk more about subs in Chapters 8 and 9.

Beyond Profit

Sometimes costs can't be controlled or are mismanaged. As costs rise, profits dwindle and may disappear altogether. In fact, some jobs may go into the hole financially before they're completed. When this happens, the job must still be completed to specifications and used to the advantage of the company. If we look at the project only as a "make money or quit" deal, we can shoot ourselves in the foot. Good advertisement comes from the satisfied client. Satisfied clients will refer you to others in a positive way. So jobs that are financial losers must still be viewed as the stepping stones to future projects—and the lead carpenter is the critical link in that stepping stones process.

After-completion surveys have taught us that the person who the client most likes and has the best feelings about is generally the lead carpenter. In short, the lead carpenter's work, attitude, demeanor, and accessibility are some of the best public relations efforts a company can make. ◿

Chapter 8

Good Job Planning

ANY SUCCESSFUL ENDEAVOR MUST START WITH GOOD PLANNING AND A REMODELING project is no exception. As you know, a lot of planning goes into drawing the plans and closing the sale. However, that will not substitute for the planning needed for the production phase of the work. This planning begins when the lead carpenter receives the plans and specs and focuses on the real work of getting the project completed on time and on budget. This chapter spells out that planning process.

TIME TO UNDERSTAND THE PROJECT

The lead carpenter should be given time to fully assess the project and digest all the paperwork before a single nail is driven or a wall is torn down. However, this orientation time is a very difficult thing to achieve for many reasons. For instance, after several months of design and spec planning, the clients want to see some action. And perhaps there is a critical ending date due to a wedding, loan date, or some other event. Moreover, the contractor is anxious to start and receive some money from the project to improve his cash flow. And the salesman is anxious to see the project start so that he can receive a commission draw.

Added to these pressures, the lead carpenter is typically just coming off a six-month project that is not quite finished. All the forces at play stand against good planning at the start of a job. But good planning can be the salvation of the job.

To repeat: The lead carpenter must be given time at the beginning of the job to review all contract documents. He must visit the site, create and review a schedule, and perform many other planning duties so that the job will flow smoothly. The lead carpenter should be compensated for this time and it should be encouraged and insisted upon by the managers.

Ideally this planning should be done on the site so that the plans can be compared to the job-site reality. Often this is impractical, however, because of clients living in the space or other factors. The next best location for job planning is in the office so that the lead has access to the salesman or contractor to answer all the questions that will come up. The lead carpenter can even do this planning at home if necessary, on company time, and sometimes a quiet home setting gives the lead carpenter the mental space he needs to fully absorb and comprehend the project. The important thing is that he be given a quiet place and the time to organize the job in his mind and on paper. The length of time needed will depend on the skills of the person and the complexity of the job, but typically takes at least a half day for an average kitchen or small addition. Remember, we can not expect anyone to walk into a job of any size and instantaneously understand all the things that have taken months for the client and salesperson to develop and understand.

First Things First

But let's back up even further. Probably even more important than understanding the project's plans and specs is achieving a basic understanding of the clients and the site. This information has probably been accumulated by the salesman in his mind, or hopefully on paper, but needs to be passed on to the carpenter so he can carry it through to the production phase of the job. The carpenter has not had the luxury of gathering this information in the course of exploratory meetings, yet he must come to the job prepared and armed with insight. This can be accomplished by having a meeting with the salesperson or by creating a form for the salesperson to fill in to be passed on as part of the job folder. Our company calls this the Job Start Checklist (Figure 13).

Getting To Know the Client

Let's start with the homeowner. A client's profession will often give us some idea of how he will react to the trauma of the remodeling experience. We must be careful not to stereotype people, but some general knowledge is often helpful. Contract lawyers, for example, will probably be very concerned about adhering to the letter of the contract. If the specs say "match existing trim," for example, they may insist that this does not mean "as close as possible with existing stock." An engineer will probably insist that all the details be precise and will often spend time in the evenings with his own tools checking your work. In these cases, you'd be wise to correct mistakes the day they happen and not wait until the next day. Architects, designers, and artists, on the other hand, will be more interested in "the look" and more time will be required for discussions and consultations in the finishing stage than in the framing stage. A little knowledge of a client's profession will affect the way in which we execute the process.

A second factor in the knowledge of the clients is to simply ask the question: Why are they doing this job? Or: What do they expect to get out of all this effort? By answering these questions you can understand which

JOB START CHECKLIST
(Received from Sales Department)

Customer: _Smith_   Contract Date: _June 10, 1998_

Salesperson: _Andy_   Start Date: _June 24, 1998_

- ☑ Plans
- ☑ Contract
- ☑ Zoning OK
- ☐ Permit *Applied for June 16, 1998–approx 2 weeks*
- ☑ "Before" photographs: Review if complete
- ☑ Review draw schedule
- ☑ Final computer spec. required
- ☐ Subcontractor and material bid

☐ Excavation *Hand Dig*	☐ Hardware
☑ Electrical	☐ Floor covering
☑ Plumbing	☑ Cabinets
☑ HVAC	☐ Wall finishes
☐ Masonry	☐ Painting
☑ Windows/Doors *WeatherShield from Peter's Window Showcase*	☐ Roofing —*Preliminary bid from Tom's Roof Covering (need to confirm)*
☐ Marble/Tile	☐ Insulation

- ☐ Items that need to be selected/approved allowances

☐ Light fixtures *Andy to follow up*	☑ Appliances
☐ Plumbing fixtures *Andy to follow up*	☐ Hardware
☐ Tile/Marble/Corian	☐ Cabinets/layout
☑ Paint color	☐ Brick
☐ Floor covering	☐ Door
☐ Shower doors *Give address to showroom*	☐ Trim detail

_____

_____

_____

_____

_____

_____

_____

_____

_____

Figure 13. Job Start Checklist

areas will be important to the clients and which will not be important. During any project, we will find items that need immediate clarification by the homeowner. However, often when these issues come up, the clients are not available. If we know the clients, and are familiar with their expectations, we will have a good idea how we should proceed.

Suppose that in the course of your planning, for instance, you find that Mr. Smith's real interest in the project is to please Mrs. Smith by providing a new kitchen. Mrs. Smith has explained that part of the reason for the new kitchen is to provide more space to eat in and to have a brighter kitchen. When the question of light placement comes up and you find duct work and beams in the places that all fifteen recessed lights are supposed to go, you will know immediately that you must call Mrs. Smith to resolve this issue. Mr. Smith probably has a passing interest and may be footing the bill, but the person with the emotional interest is Mrs. Smith. If you ask Mrs. Smith for input and to work with you, you win two people over. But if you proceed without input, you may lose the trust of two very important people in the process.

Another way that this becomes important is by noticing changes that would make the project more functional. Let's imagine that Mr. Smith really does care about the den that you are adding on because he has a rare stone collection. In your review of the job you notice that there is no lighting for the shelves in the den that will enhance the display of his collection. In the lighting walk-through this can be addressed before the drywall is done, a change order can be written, and everyone will be happy.

Hot-Button Issues

A third issue to be explored is the client's primary concerns or worries about the job. Over the years, I've found that everyone has a button that can either be massaged or pushed and it is usually under our control as to which it will be. Some people are really concerned about the job running over schedule. They have a friend that "had some work done" and the workers were there for six months past when they were welcome.

On the other hand, some people are concerned about the safety of their children, and common construction site storage practices will drive them crazy with worry. Others are concerned about the dust getting into their stereo equipment. Still others are concerned about security, so the alarm must be armed at all times, whereas the clients just a block away leave the doors unlocked all the time. Other big concerns that tend to crop up are lead paint, the neighbors' comfort, furniture protection, cost overruns, and good communication. Whatever it may be, it is important for the lead carpenter to understand the concerns of each client early in the project.

Assessing The Site

A fourth issue to address is the condition of the site. When salesmen approach the sale of a job, they try to see all the different angles and problems that will crop up. But because their primary focus is design and

ALLOWANCE/SELECTION LIST

	Selection	Allowance	OK
1. Bricks	N/A	$400 per 1,000	✔
2. Roof material	GAF		✔
3. Siding	CertainTeed-Silver fox		✔
4. Door hardware	Schlage -F-Series, Plymouth		✔
5. Plumbing fixtures	see separate sheet		✔
6. Electrical fixtures	all 1176 unless noted on plans	$750	✔
7. Wallpaper			
8. Paneling			
9. Painting	By owners		✔
10. Carpet			
11. Vinyl			
12. Ceramic tile			
13. Wood flooring			
14.			
15.			
16.			
17.			
18.			
19.			
20.			
21.			
22.			
23.			

Figure 14. Allowance Selection List

SPECIAL ORDER CHECKLIST

Item	Lead Time	Date Ordered	Date Expected	Supplier	Salesperson	Quoted Cost
Appliances	2 week	not ordered		Appliances -R-Us	Bink	$2,545
Cabinets	8 week	7/1/98	8/25/98	The Kitchen Place	Kathy	$15,263
Doors	6 week	7/14/98	8/25/98	APEX Window	Jim	$2,832
Electrical fixtures		Electrician Supplies				
Fabricate steel						
Floor covering						
Hardware (specify)						
Marble						
Medicine cabinets	1 week	Not ordered				
Millwork trim						
Plumbing fixtures						
Tile						
Tops						
Windows	6 week	7/14/98	8/25/98	APEX Window	Jim	$2,467

Figure 15. Special Order Checklist

sales, they often miss the details of how the project will actually be done. This includes the details of the site. With an eye toward productivity, the lead carpenter must see the site and ask some basic questions:

- **Parking.** Is there enough parking? Some jobs will require the presence of four to five subcontractors at one time. Where are all those trucks and cars going to sit all day? Does the neighborhood require permits for parking and, if so, who will make the arrangements to get them?
- **Deliveries.** When will there be clear access to the driveway or a similar spot for deliveries and how will that affect the scheduling and manpower needs? Does this access require that all materials be carried to the rear of the house or can they be dropped off and used off the pile as it stands?
- **Storage.** Will there be a dry place available where materials can be stored? Who is responsible for cleaning it out?
- **Utilities.** Are the utilities readily available and are they accessible in an emergency?
- **Security.** Is there a security system and will the lead carpenter be given a code or does he have to rely on the client to arm and disarm the system?
- **Landscaping.** What is the condition of the landscaping and how will it be affected by the remodeling? What promises has the salesman made about the plants and shrubs?

quote from the field

"After the walk-through... we'll figure out what material we want, which subs we want, and when we want them there. That meeting can take four hours... but it actually saves time to make sure everything's in line."

JOHN McGOWAN
Production Manager
Sass Construction, Inc.
Excelsior, Minnesota

Good Plans, Bad Plans

The next issue in this section is the status of the plans at the time of construction. We have all been in situations where the plans have been rather fluid and changes are made daily. Sometimes it is so frequent that we think we should throw away the plans and just have a meeting each day to decide what to do and what it will look like!

An understanding of the status of the plans is important for the lead carpenter. A thorough look at the plans will tell the lead if they are plans that he can actually work from. Naturally, he will find omissions and mistakes in time on any set of plans. But are the current plans really working drawings or just sketches? If they are sketches, some serious questions should be raised. Is there a copy of the plans that were approved for the permit? This has been a problem for our company in more than one instance. One set of plans went with the permit application, but in the two or three weeks that it takes to get a permit, the plans were revised, in some cases dramatically, so that when we started to build, the structure or the foundation was different. Be sure and check to see if you are building off the same set of plans as the permit set. If not, a meeting with the building inspector may be in order.

Another good question to ask is: Are there more than one set of plans in circulation? Often in remodeling, or in any construction, plans will be revised several times. In many instances the old plans are not thrown away and may still be out there in the hands of subs that are bidding the job. If the lead carpenter understands the process that the plans went through, he will stand a chance of understanding why the clients are looking at or thinking about a very different plan than he is. This will also help when a client or sub asks about an item that is not on your plans but they are sure is part of the project, only later to recall that it was eliminated on an earlier set of plans. It is critical that the lead carpenter establishes which set is the final set approved by all the parties. Finally, the lead carpenter needs to know about any last-minute revisions that are being made at the time construction begins. Management people often believe it is okay to revise the framing details while the foundation is being poured. This drives production people crazy, but as long as these changes are clearly communicated—preferably in writing—they can be worked out. Ignorance, however, is not bliss!

THE JOB FOLDER

After the site conditions have been reviewed, the lead carpenter should make a thorough check of the job folder to see if he has all the information and forms needed to complete the project. It is important that the lead carpenter has all the latest information that is available on the job at that time. The job folder should be made up by the salesman or production manager, whichever one has the information, and should contain the following:

The entire contract with the homeowner including contract price. The lead carpenter needs access to the legal conditions under which the company must work. Many companies have a standard contract which can be read and understood once and is used on every job. But on occasion it is revised to meet certain conditions for that project and the lead carpenter needs that information.

A complete set of specifications, signed by the homeowner. This may be part of the contract. The lead carpenter must have a complete set of specifications that are signed by the client so that he knows that the clients understand, or at least have signed off on, what they are getting. The lead carpenter does not have access to all the conversations that have taken place between the salesman and the clients. However, clients will typically assume that whatever the salesperson said or agreed to will be known by the lead carpenter. By everyone signing off on the specifications the lead carpenter has an agreed upon guideline from which to build.

A set of standard conditions that accompany any contract. Of course, standard conditions are not always standard and should be

PROJECT SCHEDULE

Project: _Smith_
Calendar Period: _____
Page __1__ of __1__

#	Description of Work	Aug 25	26	27	28	29	Sep 1	2	3	4	5	8	9	10	11	12	15	16	17	18	19	22	23	24	25	26	29	30	Oct 1	2	3	4
17	First floor deck	X	X																													
18	First floor walls			X	X																											
19	Second deck					X	X	X																								
20	Second floor walls								X	X																						
21	Roof and ceiling										X	X	X	X	X																	
22	Cabinet and appliance selection due									X																						
23	Install Fascia																	X														
24	Install Windows/Doors															X	X															
25	Exterior Trim																	X	X	X												
26	Stucco Siding																				X	X	X									
27	Build Powder Room Wall																				X											
28	Dust barriers/Int. Demo																				X											
29	Demo Openings to House																				X	X										
30	Roofing																						X	X								
31	Porches																								X	X	X	X				
32	Deck																												X	X	X	X

August | September | October

☐ = Projected

Figure 16. Project Schedule

PRECONSTRUCTION TOOL CHECKLIST

Job Name: _Smith_   Lead Carpenter: _Larry_

Quantity	Description	Quantity	Description
1	Air hoses		Shovel, flat
1	Air compressor		Shovel, round
	Broom, straw		Sledge hammer
1	Broom, push		Snow fence
	Caulk		Staple gun
	Change Order pad		Tape, duct
	Construction adhesive		Tape, masking
	Demo hammer		Time cards
1	Framing gun		Transit _be sure and bring tripod too_
	Hammer drill		Trash can
	Jack hammer		Weekly reports
1	Knack box		Wheelbarrow
1	Ladder, step _6 ft._		Nails (list type) _12d gun,_
	Ladder, extension		_5lbs–12d sinkers_
	Lights _–with 25ft wire_		_8d gun_
	Masonite		Saw blades (list type)
	Phone box		
1	Phone		
	Pick		Special hardware (list type)
	Plastic _1 large bundle_		
	Ramset		
	Rosin paper		Other:
	Scaffolding		
1	Shims		
	Shop vac		

Figure 17. Preconstruction Tool Checklist

reviewed by the lead carpenter on each job. Items included are: use of utilities, standard hourly rate for time and material charges, hidden condition clauses, etc.

Current plans that can be used to build the project. The need to have up-to-date plans is obvious and the lead carpenter should have at least two sets to start with.

Any permits needed to complete the project, including building, parking, public space usage (for a dumpster), historical review, etc. Any permits needed for the job should be given to the lead carpenter before the job starts and posted on the site.

A list of all selections that have not been made to date. This list (Figure 14) enables the lead carpenter to see at a glance if he should start reminding someone about a selection that needs to be made. A common mistake is to believe that plumbing fixtures can be selected near the end of the job. If the lead carpenter knows before the job starts that the shower valve is not selected and he knows that the rough-in inspection will be only three weeks from start, he can start talking to the right people about making a decision quickly.

List of special-order items with lead times. This is a list of all the items that are included in the project which the lead carpenter probably doesn't know about, e.g., a new form of siding that will have to be ordered or special brick or block that takes three weeks to get but is needed early in the job. Any item that the salespeople have sold that will require a lead time should be written down to provide the lead carpenter with the information to order properly and in time for the work (Figure 15). The list should include the complete item description, the supplier to order from, the salesperson's name to order from, the quoted cost, and the lead time.

A complete estimate of all phases of the job. The lead carpenter should be given a complete estimate of the project. This estimate will enable him to make intelligent choices about what materials to use, the schedule of the job and manpower usage, and to have a better understanding of the costs of doing business. The estimate should be complete and accurate.

A schedule or a schedule form. The lead carpenter should be responsible for filling in or making a schedule (Figure 16). The lead carpenter, after careful study, is really the only person who can tell how this job will progress and should therefore make the schedule. It is always easier to do this if there is a standardized form where the blanks can be filled in so that there is nothing omitted.

Subcontract agreements for all subs as needed for the job. Ideally, all the subs have been selected for a job before the lead carpenter receives the paperwork, so all contracts from subs should be in the file. In reality, it doesn't always work that way. If there is no contract for a particular phase, a note about which sub to call for that work should be included. At any rate, the lead carpenter should end up with a copy of all contracts with subcontractors. This enables him to see exactly what the

JOB SITE ASSESSMENT FORM

Job Name: _Smith_   Contract #: _306_   Date: _7/14/98_

Section 1. Site Prep

Locate:
- ☑ Trash pile
- ☑ Lockbox
- ☑ Bathroom
- ☑ Material storage, interior
- ☑ Material storage, exterior

- ☑ Landscape protection
- ☑ Parking
- ☑ Job phone
- ☑ Dust protection assessed
- ☑ Floor protection assessed
- ☑ Furniture/breakables to be removed

Section 2: Site Conditions

☑ **Wall finish condition:** _Good-all areas that are water damaged will be removed in construction_

☑ **Floor condition:** _Good_

☑ **Ceiling condition:** _Same as wall finish_

☑ **Windows & doors condition:** _2 of windows that remain have broken sash cords-do not open properly_

☑ **Trim condition:** _Good shape-appear to be 2¼ Colonial._
Contract calls for 2¼ clam shell-is this a conflict?

☑ **Bath fixtures:** _No cracks that I can see_

    Water supply: _Good_

    Drain: _Drains well_

    Finishes:

☑ **Kitchen – Cabinets:** _Good_

    Water supply: _Good_

    Drain: _Good-sink is scratched a little_

    Countertops: _Good shape_

    Appliances: _Good_

☑ **Driveway condition:** _One corner of drive has a crack_

☑ **Landscaping:** _Smiths have moved all affected shrubs_

Figure 18. Job Site Assessment Form (continued on next page)

Section 3. Site Survey *(continued)*

1. Basement/Foundation: _Generally ok_   Type: _Concrete_

   Condition:

   Finish: _None_   Moist: _a little_

   Height: _7'10"_   Plumb: _ok_

2. Attic: _Not insulated_   Type: _____

   Condition:

   Rafters: _2x8_   Joists: _2x6_

                                     Utilities: _HVAC unit_

3. Roof: _Generally Good-a few rough spots_   Type: _Asphalt shingle_

   Condition:

   Gutters: _Good_   Water protection? _good_

   Soffit: _Good_   Fascia: _good_

4. Floors: Alignment (level?) _Workable_   Finish condition: _____

5. Trim: Baseboard type: _1x4 with cap_   Size: _1x4 with 1⅝" cap_

   Casing type: _Colonial_   Size: _2¼_

6. Doors & Windows: Door: _wood-brass w.s._   Head height: _6'8"_

   Window: _DH with weights_   Head height: _6'10"_

                                     Sill height: _3'4"_

Lead Carpenter: _Larry the Lead_   Date: _7/14/98_

I have read this Job Site Assessment and agree with its contents.

Owner: _John Smith_   Date: _7/14/98_

Owner: _Mary Smith_   Date: _7/14/98_

Figure 18. Job Site Assessment Form (continued from previous page)

WEEKLY TIME CARD

Name: _Larry the Lead_   Week Ending: _6/20/99_

Day	Job	Description	Code	Start	Stop	Hours
Wed 4	Smith	Framing first floor wall	6	7⁰⁰	12⁰⁰	5
		Client meeting	1	12³⁰	2⁰⁰	1.5
		Framing 2nd floor deck	6	2⁰⁰	3⁰⁰	1
Lunch ½ hr		Admin	1	3⁰⁰	3³⁰	.5
Thurs 5	Smith	Frame 2nd floor deck and				
		2nd floor walls	6	7⁰⁰	3⁰⁰	7.5
		Admin	1	3⁰⁰	3³⁰	.5
Lunch ½ hr						
Fri 6	Smith	Meet plumber to review layout	1	7⁰⁰	8³⁰	1.5
		Roof framing	6	8³⁰	3⁰⁰	6
		Admin	1	3⁰⁰	3³⁰	.5
Lunch ½ hr						
Mon 7	Smith	Calculate and order all siding & trim	1	7⁰⁰	8⁰⁰	1
		Site meeting with Boss	1	8⁰⁰	9³⁰	1.5
		Frame roof	6	9³⁰	3⁰⁰	5.5
Lunch ½ hr		Admin	1	3⁰⁰	3³⁰	.5
Tues 8	Smith	Frame roof	6	7⁰⁰	12⁰⁰	5
	Jones	Returned for warranty work	28	12³⁰	3³⁰	3
Lunch ½ hr						

Figure 19. Weekly Time Card

sub is responsible for on the job and will eliminate some of the confusion that typically occurs around who is responsible for what.

Preconstruction tool checklist. This list, created by the contractor and/or the lead carpenter, should include all materials or tools that need to be delivered to the site before the carpenter arrives, so that when he arrives he can start working (Figure 17). Items on this list may include plastic for projections, shovels, nails, saw blades, storage boxes, etc. The list can be used by the lead to check off items that he will need delivered to the site while he is finishing the current project. This allows him to hit the ground running when he arrives.

Job-site assessment form. This checklist systematically covers the existing condition of all areas that may be affected by the work to establish their condition before work starts (Figure 18). This checks the existing house for defects that will and will not be corrected as part of the contract. This also gives the lead carpenter the opportunity to carefully examine the home to see if floors are level, walls are plumb, and outlets work, and to make adjustments ahead of time instead of finding later that walls and floors don't line up. Every contractor has ended up making repairs to a home that were not part of the contract, but which seemed to appear during the project. Some of these may not even be in the remodeled areas of the house.

Time sheets for reporting labor hours. An easy-to-use time sheet (Figure 19) is critical for accurate job costing. Getting other carpenters and helpers to fill these in is an important responsibility of the lead carpenter.

Job logs for tracking the activity of the job. Job logs should include a place for the lead carpenter's name, the job name, date, other employees on the site, subs on the job, weather conditions, work accomplished for that day, and a lengthy place for notes (Figure 20). The reason the form is so important is for recording what does take place in case there are disputes about the job. If a client gives the lead carpenter the go ahead to make a change, he can write it down. If the lead is walking through with the sub and they see a change that must be made, he can write it down. In each case the lead will be able to recall the conversation more accurately with notes than without notes.

Change order forms for use in the field. If lead carpenters are involved in executing change orders in your company, they should have a form to help with that work (Figure 21). Because forgotten or incomplete or unsigned change orders can cause a company a lot of grief and money, extra attention should be given to this issue. The forms should be clear, and training sessions on how to complete the forms should occur regularly.

List of client responsibilities. Whatever the clients are responsible for should be documented in written form. If they agree to move out all belongings by a certain date, it should be written down so the lead knows about it. If they agree to open the door every morning at 6:30 a.m., it should be written down so that everyone knows it. The produc-

EVERYDAY CONSTRUCTION
Job Log

Project: _Smith_   Weather: ☑ Fair   ☐ Overcast   ☐ Rain   ☐ Snow

Job Number: _324_   Temperature: ☐ 0-30   ☐ 30-50   ☐ 50-60   ☑ 60&up

Lead Carpenter: _Larry_   Wind: ☑ Still   ☐ Moderate   ☐ High

___Excavators	___Plumbers	___Security/Audio	___Carpet Installers
___Footings	___Electricians	___Stone Masons	___Vinyl Installers
___Block Work	___Heat & A/C	___Gutters & Downspouts	___Cntrtop Installers
___Exterminators	___Insulators	___Hardwood Installers	___Mirror/Shwr/Hdwr.
_I_ Laborers	___Roofers	___Ceram. Tile Installer	___Driveway Installers
___Conc. Flatwork	___Drywallers	___Trim Carpenters	___Cleaners
___Frame Carpent.	___Brick Layers	___Painters	___Landscapers
___St. Fabricators	___Siding Installer	___Special Millwork	___Others_____

Visitors: (i.e., Homeowner, Architect, Office Personnel, Construction Manager)

Time	Name	Remarks
_____	_____	_____
_____	_____	_____
_____	_____	_____

Hopkins & Porter Labor:

Name	Time		Total Hrs	Rate	Cost	Item Code/ Work Completed
Larry Lead	7⁰⁰	to 3³⁰	8	25	200⁰⁰	Framing
Harry Helper	7⁰⁰	to 3³⁰	8	12	96	Framing
_____	___	to ___	_____	_____	_____	_____
_____	___	to ___	_____	_____	_____	_____
_____	___	to ___	_____	_____	_____	_____

Total Cost:_____   Cumulative:_____   Budget:_____

Homeowner Remarks: _____

Extra Work/Changes Requested by Homeowner: _____ _John Smith requested we move a window—_
CO form send in office

Selections/Decisions to be made by Homeowner: _____
_____ by (Date):_____

Daily Notes: _1) Use temp labor in basement while Harry & I frame_
2) set up plumber to come by and look at potential problem
_____
_____
_____
_____

Reviewed by supervisor:_____ Date:_____

Figure 20. Daily Job Log

STIPULATED SUM
Change Order #___1___

Job Name & Number: ___Smith 302___   Date: ___7/14/98___

Prepared By: ___Larry the Lead___

Change Description Note: Please use Sub name	Phase #	Labor hours x $	Material Cost	Sub Cost/ Name	Total Cost	M.U. @ 20%	Sale Price
Change the location	Framing	6 x 49.00 294	75.00	—	369	74.00	443.00
of bath room window							
to be beside door.							
Add two recessed	Framing	3 x 49.00 147	30.00		177	35.00	212.00
lights to center on	Electrical		75.00	100.00	175	35.00	210.00
window							
							422.00

Labor Charge: Lead Carpenter @ . . . . . $49.00   # of Days:_____   Total:_____

                    Helper @ $40.00

Date entered into Computer: #21_____

                            #94_____

Figure 21a. Change Order

FIELD CHANGE ORDER

We agree to make change(s) or perform additional work at the request and orders of:

Name	Smith	Date: June 30, 1998
Address	100 Fiarhaven Lane	Job #: 226
City, State, Zip Code	Parisville, OH	Date of Existing Contract:
Job Address	Same	Job Phone:

hereinafter referred to as Owner, for work performed at premises set forth above. It is proposed to make changes(s) or perform additional work as follows:

Move window in East wall three feet to the left to accommodate a

new dresser

Requires 10 addition 2x8x8

1 4x7x1/2

16 man hours

Additional work specified above becomes part of and is to be performed under the same conditions as the existing contract between Contractor and Owner when signed Change Order is received by Contractor.

Larry Lead	6/30/92	John Smith	6/30/92
Company Representative	Date	Owner	Date

Figure 21b. Field Change Order

tion crew often gets stuck because the client's role in the process is left undefined. This vagueness can be eliminated by good paperwork.

Material take off form. This form helps the lead carpenter create a complete materials list from the plans. This process is described in detail in the next section of this chapter.

After the lead carpenter has checked through the job file, he should report any missing items that he needs and get some kind of commitment from the office about when he will receive them. He should then take company time to fill in all the forms and review each document in the file. This may take as long as a full day, but will be worth the time when you average it out over the several weeks or months the job will be running smoothly.

MATERIAL TAKEOFFS

Good planning involves making a complete material list before the job begins. Many carpenters think this is a waste of time for the simple reason that in some cases you can't know exactly what you need until a wall is torn down or a foundation is built. In some cases it is foolish to expect the plans to be accurate enough to order materials from them. But there are some good, economical reasons to develop a list beforehand regardless of the site conditions.

Mainly, the material list is an important planning tool for the lead carpenter. By reviewing the plans and site conditions thoroughly ahead of time in order to make the list, he has one more assurance that the job has been reviewed from top to bottom. It also helps in the search for any special-order items that have not already been identified, and allows the lead carpenter to find out about the availability and lead time for these items. Often the flagging of a special-order item allows the carpenter to see what other materials or steps in the job must be completed before that item can be properly ordered.

Making this list ahead of time also allows the lead carpenter to make good choices about materials. Suppose a specification does not detail the kind of exterior trim to use. The takeoff list allows the carpenter an opportunity to decide what the best application for this job will be, perhaps D and better, finger-joint pine or fir, redwood, ply trim, and the list goes on.

The material list also gives the carpenter the opportunity to shop the materials to several suppliers. When a supplier sees a list for a whole job come through, he will be more likely to give you a discount than he would for a piecemeal order. Lumber prices are very fluid and suppliers' prices should be checked on a regular basis. It may be the difference in producing the job on the budget or over the budget. A carefully prepared list will also allow you to plan and order your deliveries in a way that fits the site conditions as well as your scheduling needs.

Generating a material list is something that most people reading this book have done, but we will discuss it for the novices and maybe the experts will pick up a tip or two. Start with the very first task you have to do and work through the job step by step in your mind. (It may be a good idea to do your schedule at the same time.) Write down all the materials that you will need to complete each phase of the work. This includes disposable blades and bits, string chalk, 2x4s, everything. This process should occur with the plans and specifications open in front of you so that you can cross reference each. (This is another time when you may discover conflicts between the plan and specifications. Write those down and get them clarified before the job begins.)

Your list should be made in a notebook that will remain on the job for future reference. Be sure to consider waste factors in your estimates. The lead on each job will be the only one who can figure this out. Each person has his own way to figure waste factors for the way he works. This process is not foolproof but will allow the lead carpenter to have a list to work from as the job progresses. This will save time and money in the long run both in ordering materials and in dealing with plan and specification inconsistencies before they become an expensive problem.

PRECONSTRUCTION MEETING

Proper planning involves a preconstruction conference with all the parties involved in the job—the lead carpenter, salesperson, production manager, clients (both, if a couple), etc.

Up to this time, the clients have been working with one or perhaps two of these people in the design/sales phase and need the opportunity to meet and become familiar with the rest of the team. Not only do the clients need this chance to learn about the lead carpenter (the person who will share their house with them for the next three or four months), but the lead carpenter needs the chance to meet and learn about the clients (the people who will be reviewing and critiquing his work for the next three or four months).

If, for any reason, the lead carpenter can't attend this meeting, it is imperative that he find a time to meet with the clients separately. One way to handle this is to set up a meeting at the site as soon as the lead carpenter is available. The worst scenario for the clients would be for a complete stranger to show up one morning and start working on their house.

The preconstruction meeting is essential and accomplishes several goals. First, it allows the clients and lead carpenter to meet each other and lets the lead carpenter take over as the client's primary contact point within the company. This one meeting really isn't sufficient to fully "pass the baton" from the salesperson to the lead carpenter and to address all the issues that will arise on the job, but it is a start in the right direction. The contractor can ease this transition by introducing the lead, giving

PRECONSTRUCTION MEETING CHECKLIST

Job Name: _Smith_   Date: _June 17, 1998_

People Present: _John & Pam Smith_

Things to take to meeting:

Stamped plans
Business cards
Specs and Contract

1. Purpose of meeting: Introduce entire "team."

2. What do clients expect from the project? From us? _Timely finish, special party Sept 26_

3. Any special considerations for clients? Other people to be aware of? _4 year old son, Jonathan_

4. Inform clients of dust, dirt, noise, inconvenience. Discuss.

5. Everyday issues:

   a. Job hours: 7 a.m. – 3:30 p.m.

   b. Bathroom

   c. Keys/security

   d. Telephone

   e. Trash

   f. Job sign

   g. Location of utilities (please clear access)

   h. Change Order policy (takes time, slows job, signed forms)

   i. List of salvage items

   j. Emergency pager number _(301-555-5555)_

   k. Smoking policy

   l.

   m.

   n.

   o.

   p.

Phone Numbers

His Work: _301-555-1212_
Her Work: _202-555-1212_
Home: _410-555-1212_

6. Selections that still need to be made:

   a. _Smith is not clear on the window casing detail–need to get them a sample_

   b. _Tile needs to be selected –sales person will work with Smith on this_

   c. _____

   d. _____

   e. _____

   f. _____

7. Start date and what happens between now and then:

8. Discuss importance of GOOD COMMUNICATION!

9. Tour of home.

Figure 22. Preconstruction Meeting Checklist

some background on the lead (years in the trades, years with the company, projects he has completed that the client may have seen) and indicating verbally his trust in the lead's ability. A trained lead can then run the remainder of the meeting and begin building the trust of the client.

Second, this is an ideal time to ask all the questions raised during the lead carpenter's review of the plans and specifications. A quick review of the specifications is in order, with particular attention to areas that are not clear or that raise warning flags. A review of the plans is important as well with an eye toward clarifying details that are unclear. Now is also the time to get clarification on conflicts between plans and specs and to clearly establish which is the final set of plans to build from. Also, use this time to review fixture selections—particularly which items have been selected, which still need to be chosen, and when you need to have that information.

Although the clients, as well as the salesperson, have been looking at these plans and specifications for months, they will probably not be aware of construction details or technical difficulties from the perspective of the production staff. Raising these questions, therefore, does require a certain amount of trust between the salespeople and the lead carpenter but it is critical for the success of the job. Not only is this a good time for questions about the plans and specs, but it is also an ideal time to ask about the clients' expectations and to ferret out their hot buttons. What are their expectations? What brought about this project? What aspects of the project are most important to them? Use this time to figure out what makes these people tick and how the lead carpenter can help them tick more happily. A preconstruction meeting form or checklist (Figure 22) can be helpful in remembering to address everything that needs addressing in this meeting.

This meeting is also the time to establish the daily job procedures which may include:
• Starting and stopping time for each day
• Phone use, bathroom use
• Trash pile or dumpster location
• Access to the site
• Care of pets; children to be aware of
• Smoking policy
• Clients' allergies
• Radio use
• Security and use of clients' key
• Any other client concerns or questions

Further, the lead carpenter should explain how he expects the job to progress. The lead should consult with the salesperson before the meeting to see what has been promised, but the lead carpenter needs to have control of the schedule and be able to give the client milestones to anticipate. When will the wall demo be done? How long will the kitchen be out of commission? When will they be able to use the new whirlpool or

HOPKINS & PORTER CONSTRUCTION
JOB NAME: JONES

*NOTE: DDD DATES (DROP DEAD DATES) ARE CRITICAL TO THE TIMELY SUCCESS OF THE PROJECT.

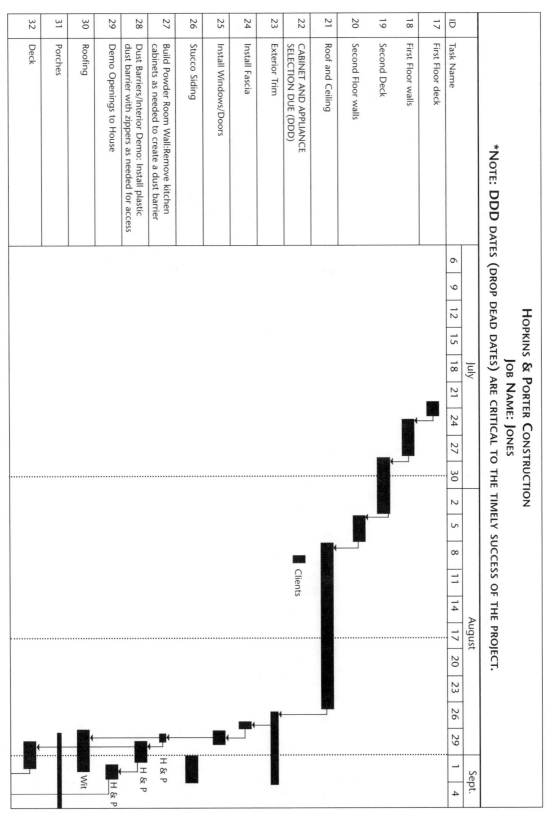

ID	Task Name
17	First Floor deck
18	First Floor walls
19	Second Deck
20	Second Floor walls
21	Roof and Ceiling
22	CABINET AND APPLIANCE SELECTION DUE (DDD)
23	Exterior Trim
24	Install Fascia
25	Install Windows/Doors
26	Stucco Siding
27	Build Powder Room Wall:Remove kitchen cabinets as needed to create a dust barrier
28	Dust Barriers/Interior Demo: Install plastic dust barrier with zippers as needed for access
29	Demo Openings to House
30	Roofing
31	Porches
32	Deck

Figure 23. Job Schedule: Microsoft Project Format

PROJECT SCHEDULE: LIST FORMAT

Job Name: *Smith*   Lead Carpenter: *Larry*

ID	Task Name	Duration	Start	Finish	Predecessors	Resource Names
1	Review Plans and Estimate	5d	Mon 11/10/97	Fri 11/14/98		
2	Meeting at Hopkins & Porter	1d	Thu 11/20/97	Thu 11/20/97		
3	Draw final drawing	60d	Fri 11/21/97	Thu 2/12/98	2	
4	Draw permit set	6w	Fri 11/21/97	Thu 1/1/98	1	
5	Draw final	30d	Fri 1/2/98	Thu 2/12/98	4	
6	Apply for permit	8w	Fri 1/2/98	Thu 2/26/98	4	
7	Begin excavation	3d	Fri 2/27/98	Tue 3/3/98	6	
8	Foundation work	2w	Wed 3/4/98	Tue 3/17/98	7	
9	Waterproofing	1d	Wed 3/18/98	Wed 3/18/98	8	
10	Foundation Inspection	1d	Thu 3/19/98	Thu 3/19/98	9	
11	Backfill	2d	Fri 3/20/98	Mon 3/23/98	10	
12	Framing	8w	Tue 3/24/98	Mon 5/18/98	11	
13	Exterior Trim	2w	Tue 5/19/98	Mon 6/1/98	12	
14	Rough In Trades	20d	Tue 5/19/98	Mon 6/15/98		
15	HVAC	2w	Tue 5/19/98	Mon 6/1/98	12	
16	Plumbing	1w	Tue 6/2/98	Mon 6/8/98	15	
17	Electrical	1w	Tue 6/9/98	Mon 6/15/98	16	
18	Inspection	1d	Tue 6/16/98	Tue 6/16/98	17	
19	Insulation	3d	Wed 6/17/98	Fri 6/19/98	18	
20	Drywall	3w	Mon 6/22/98	Fri 7/10/98	19	
21	Interior Doors	2d	Mon 7/13/98	Tue 7/14/98	20	
22	Interior Cabinets	2d	Wed 7/15/98	Thu 7/16/98	21	
23	Interior trim	3w	Fri 7/17/98	Thu 8/6/98	22	
24	Install Wood Floors	2w	Fri 8/7/98	Thu 8/20/98	23	
25	Interior Paint	4w	Fri 8/21/98	Thu 9/17/98	24	
26	Carpets	1w	Fri 9/18/98	Thu 9/24/98	25	
27	Cleaning	2d	Fri 9/25/98	Mon 9/28/98	26	

Figure 24. Project Schedule: List Format

hot tub? And, last but not least, when will the job be finished? Do not be afraid to talk about the schedule, but be realistic. The saying goes: "Under-promise, over-deliver."

Finally, a review of the change order policy is important at this meeting. Most clients will say that they have looked at the plans and there will be no changes. But those of us who have been around know that this is rarely true. It is important to establish exactly what should happen when a change order is necessary. You should also point out the line on the change order form that specifies the new completion date as a result of the change. If clients know in advance that changes will make the job last longer, they might be less impulsive about making alterations to the original plan.

SCHEDULING

Good planning involves the use of an often misunderstood and under-used tool: the schedule. Most carpenters believe there is no benefit to having a schedule since very rarely are they followed. Some carpenters consider schedules an insult to their integrity. This stems from a belief that the schedule is there to make them work harder or faster by creating unrealistic ending dates. The fact is that most lead carpenters do work as hard as they can, so the purpose of the schedule is to help them and others work smarter.

Still, the question is often asked: Why do a schedule? To answer this, the lead carpenter must change his perspective. Most carpenters come at a project as a work of art that they must produce to their standard of quality. We must change our frame of reference and come at the project as something that must be completed within the budget established by the clients and the salesperson. This change of reference can be seen very clearly in which materials are specified. All carpenters I know would rather use an all-wood door instead of a composite door. However, there are price differences and if the client is buying a composite door as defined in the contract, despite my personal definition of quality, I am not at liberty to change the plan.

The same is true with regard to the time frame and the cost of the job. Granted, there is a certain amount of time needed to do basic parts of any project, but we are also aware that by devoting more time to any part of the project, it can be made closer to perfection. But is perfection of the job—without sufficient financial support from the client—our moral duty? Not in the business world. We must adjust our thinking to ask the question: "What level of perfection will the budget allow?" To do this we must make a schedule based on the budget as well as our perception of the time required to complete the job.

Establishing a written job schedule helps put labor dollars onto paper. Before beginning to write down how many days it will take to complete a given task, take the labor budgets and divide by the cost per hour for that labor. Then take these numbers and turn them into corresponding days. Let's say you have $3,597 for labor to complete the framing on a project. It will cost you $36/hour for yourself and a helper to do the work and there are eight hours in a work day. So one day of labor will cost $288. You divide $3,597 by $288 ($36/hr x 8) to tell you that you have 12.48 days to complete the framing. This kind of schedule may not seem realistic, but it will tell you the time frame you have for completing the project within the budget.

The dollar cost of overruns. Another reason for creating a schedule is that overruns on jobs create losses in overhead and profit.

Let's look at losses in overhead:

If yearly sales equal	$750,000.00
Then monthly sales equal	$62,500.00 ($750,000 ÷ 12)
Then monthly overhead at 20% is	$12,500.00 ($62,000 x .20)
Daily overhead (20 work days) is	$612.00 ($12,500 ÷ 20)
Daily overhead per job with 2 jobs running is	$312.50 ($625.00÷ 2)

If a job goes over schedule, the company begins to lose $312.50 per day in overhead that could be allocated to a new job.

Now let's look at losses in profit:

If yearly sales equal	$750,000.00
Then yearly profit at 10% equals	$75,000.00 ($750,000 x.10)
Then monthly profit equals	$6,250.00 ($75,000÷ 12)
Then daily profit (20 work days) is	$312.50 ($6,250.00÷20)
Daily profit per job with 2 jobs running is	$156.25 ($312.50÷2)

If a job goes over schedule, the company begins to lose $156.25 per day in profit. If you add that to one day's worth of lost overhead ($312.50), you find that going over the schedule by just one day costs the company $468.75, not counting the labor costs incurred that day!

An ounce of prevention. Another reason to do a schedule is to address potential problems before they become real problems. The fundamental question must be asked, "Can this project be built for the budget you have been given?" If the answer is no, then plans need to be made to retrieve some of that cost overrun and/or work the job in a different way.

Some other questions to ask during the scheduling process are:
1) Are there any trades needed for the job and on the schedule that are not represented in the budget?
2) What special-order items need to be ordered and how do their availability affect the schedule?
3) Is there a time in the project that the lead carpenter needs to be off

the job and assigned to another job? (Although the ideal is for the lead carpenter to stay on the job at all times, this schedule dilemma may come around and needs to be addressed.)

4) When will the job be finished (when will the lead carpenter be ready for another job) and are the salespeople working on a project that they can move to at that time?

In short, a schedule will give the lead carpenter the opportunity to think the job through and address timing issues before they create problems.

The how-to of scheduling. With the questions of "why" answered, we turn to the questions of "how." Using a standardized form and filling in the blanks is the best way to approach this. It helps to keep the scheduler from forgetting areas of work that are not obvious. This form can be a bar graph (Figure 23), a list of tasks (Figure 24), or a calendar to fill in. As the lead is working through the form he can consider manpower needs. If a task can be done with one person, that is usually the best and most efficient approach and should be scheduled for enough days and money for one person. However, if the job requires two or three people, the schedule should reflect those dollars and that time frame.

This is another part of the planning that requires thinking through the job from beginning to end. This can be done at the same time as the material list to save on time and effort. Refer to the job specifications as you go so that everything will be covered. There are times, as mentioned before, that the plans or specifications are missing a detail, so if both are consulted the whole picture should emerge.

Use the estimate to understand the labor dollar values for each part of the project as described in the previous section. It is important to consider in the process the tasks that are concurrent and the tasks that are consecutive. For example, drywall hanging is always dependent on the completion of the rough-in of the trades. They are consecutive tasks. Roofing or siding, however, can be done before, after, or during rough-in of the trades. They will be concurrent or consecutive depending on the project. There are commonly accepted rules for scheduling—for example, HVAC is completed, then plumbing, then electric. To make a project work, there are times when the rules need to be stretched or broken. This will be dependent on the size of the job and the space available.

In a whole-house renovation, many people can work in the space at the same time. In a small kitchen renovation, on the other hand, the trades will have to work one at a time. To account for these variations, make the schedule as detailed as you can and still usable. Include order dates, milestones that must be met, inspections, and end dates. The key to a successful schedule is to update it regularly. This can be done on the same paper as the actual vs. real costs, but with a different color ink to track the actual vs. real dates. In addition to the job schedule, lead carpenters should use a weekly schedule to facilitate detailed day-by-day planning. ◪

Chapter 9

Site Supervision

In the next stage of the project, the role of the lead carpenter becomes highly visible. The actual construction work has started and the management work of the lead enters a new, more interactive, phase. He now becomes the supervisor of the process that will lead to a completed project. The completion of the project is never in doubt. However, the satisfaction and happiness of all the people involved hangs in the balance. What the lead carpenter does now will determine the outcome of the project for many people.

The lead carpenter must supervise every aspect of the job—from the ordering, delivery, and quality control of all materials to the supervision of all manpower on the job. While working with his supervisor, whether that's the contractor or the production manager, the lead carpenter must learn effective ways to manage the flow of work as well as the people on the job, to maximize profitability. This should include the training of other employees who will become lead carpenters.

Safety has become one of the major concerns of any construction company for both health and financial reasons, and the lead must be responsible for on-site compliance with company rules. The lead carpenter must have a working knowledge of where potential hazards are and how to use safe practices to protect against accidents. He must also be prepared to insist on safe practices.

The on-site supervision of subcontractors by the lead carpenter is a benefit to both the contractor and the subcontractor. The lead must have the ability to schedule and work with the subs on the job. He should also have at least a passing familiarity with his area's codes covering each sub-trade.

This chapter discusses the distinct areas where a lead carpenter really takes the lead.

SUPERVISION OF MATERIALS

You'd expect that supervision of materials would be second nature to anyone who has worked in construction very long. Some of the ideas set out in this section will be too basic for many readers, but some may add a practical tip that will turn a difficult job into an easy job.

Ordering Materials

Start the ordering process with the list of materials that was created in the planning stages of the project. Verify that the quantities are still accurate. Consider the lead time of each item. Be sure you have a good understanding of how long it will take for your supplier to obtain your materials. Many items will be on hand, but others have to be ordered and shipped to the supplier. Whenever you encounter an item that you have never used before, check the lead time. Architects, clients, and sales people have a habit of specifying something without knowing the availability. Clients have told me a ceramic tile is "in stock." What that means, however, is that it is in a warehouse in Topeka, Kansas, and can be shipped to me in two weeks!

Carefully consider delivery time, which is the time it takes your supplier to bring the material to you from its yard. When work is slow, you may be able to get next-day delivery. When work is booming, it may take two or three days. And what does "next-day delivery" mean, anyway? By 7:00 a.m. the next day or sometime before the yard closes at 6:00 p.m.? This becomes an important consideration when you have two or three people waiting to help with framing and the lumber is not there.

Consider manpower and what you can accomplish in x amount of time. Remodeling sites are often small areas and space is a big consideration. Think about how much material your crew can consume in the time between deliveries. If you order too much, there will be a problem with space, and time and money will be wasted tripping over the excess piles. If you order too little, people will be standing around with nothing to do while someone runs to pick up a stack of 2x4s. This creates a double waste of money. Order a quantity that can be stored easily on site. It would be nice if the materials that we needed could be delivered all at one time. But space rarely allows us this luxury. So we must think about how to store this material and how fast we will use it.

Quality Control

The lead carpenter is responsible for checking the materials that are delivered to the site to assure their quality. Here are a few suggestions in this regard:

- ***Keep your order list*** to be sure everything that you ordered has been delivered. The purpose of a list written on paper, not a 2x4, is clear here. There is nothing more frustrating than discovering that items have been back-ordered or omitted.

- **Do not rely on the delivery ticket** to check the accuracy of the order. All the delivery ticket tells you is what they claim to have brought you and what you will be billed for. Check everything that is delivered against the delivery ticket. If you accept the order as written on the delivery ticket, that is what you pay for.
- **Send back whatever is defective or unusable.** If an item delivered is unusable by your standards, leave it on the truck, make a note on the ticket, and let them take it back right then. If you accept it and try to return it later, you will forget it or damage it, and end up paying for it in the long run. Let suppliers know when material is defective or if you have delivery problems. The only way to correct problems in delivery is to tell the people who are responsible about your complaints. In today's business environment, service is a big consideration in who gets our business. Suppliers know this and will respond to your needs.
- **Check the order to be sure reordered items match original materials.** If you are reordering trim or moldings, check the profiles to be sure they match the original style. Sometimes lumberyards will change suppliers in mid-job and the profile will be slightly different.
- **Be sure paperwork is in order.** Save all your paperwork, including receipts, delivery tickets, and return tickets. If questions arise about a delivery or what happened to an order, accurate paperwork always settles the question.

SUPERVISING EMPLOYEES

The supervision of inanimate objects is easy compared to the supervision of fellow employees. For many lead carpenters this is the hardest part of the job. It goes far beyond simply assigning tasks to everyone and letting them do their thing. It requires diplomacy, tact, patience, and optimism, as well as a good knowledge of human nature.

Good supervision of employees involves three basic areas:
1) Proper crew size for efficiency and profitability,
2) Division of labor, and
3) Motivating people.

When all three of these areas are given the proper attention, you'll get maximum results. If one area is lacking, however, only partial supervision is achieved.

Proper crew size. Traditionally, in construction, a crew is made up of a foreman and one or two helpers. This crew stays together and moves from job to job as a unit. This concept works well for large construction projects where there is always useful work for those people to do. The unit members learn how each other works, they develop a routine for unpacking and packing tools, breaks are handled the same each day, and a level of efficiency is maintained.

However, in remodeling where lead carpenters are used primarily, the dynamics of the work place are different. Many projects are small, in both cost and scale. There are times when nothing except planning can or should be done. There is a client that needs attention. The flow of the job is different. Framing for shoring may occur before the foundation is dug and then again after the foundation is laid. For these and other reasons, it often makes sense to break up the three-man crew and work with what we call "the one-man crew." I'll explain this more fully in the next section.

Division of labor. There has to be one person who takes responsibility for the project and in this case it's the lead carpenter assigned to the job. Even if there are more than one lead carpenter working on the project, only one is in charge. What this means is that he must seize control of the resources available and put them to work. In this regard, there are two main objectives: production and training.

The lead carpenter's main task is to produce a product. This must be kept in mind when the tasks are being handed out. The lead may like being the cut man for roof framing, but more important is figuring out the strengths and weaknesses of each worker. How can the labor be split up to be most efficient? It will not surprise anyone to know that it is not always the way people like it. In some cases, it helps to split the job up into small one-man crews. Assign one person to trim all the windows, another to run the base. By doing this, you reap some of the benefits of the one-man crew. This also means that the lead carpenter must say how he wants the work done. The lead carpenter will be the only person on the job that has all the details of the job in mind and can accurately direct how things ought to be done.

I have worked on jobs where I really felt the lead carpenter was wrong about a trim detail, but I did it his way. (I would draw the line on a structural problem, or something that was unsafe, but in general I do it his way.) He is responsible to management for his decisions.

A secondary task for the lead carpenter is to provide training for other carpenters and helpers. In managing the crew, a decision should be made about training and how it should be done. This can be done by working with the individual or by letting him loose and checking his work later. Either approach can be made to work and needs to be adapted to each person.

Motivating people. At times, we have all run into people who have the talent, the tools, and the knowledge to do anything they want, but lack motivation. Sometimes workers on our jobs don't come to work ready to produce but rather are there to make it through the day and collect a paycheck. Still others come prepared to work, but with a little extra push, could accomplish much more than they usually do. The task of motivating employees on the site falls to the lead carpenter. Here are some tips that I have found to be extremely effective:

Be enthusiastic. Your own attitude is perhaps the greatest influence of all. It sets the tone for the entire crew. If you come in complaining, expect the same in return. If you come in optimistic, it may take some time, but you'll get it in return. If you have a can-do attitude, others will pick it up.

Delegate tasks. People thrive on being trusted. This is particularly true of people who are learning a trade. They will try extra hard if given a task to complete by themselves. Be sure and check the work, critique the progress, and give feedback, both praise and correction.

Work beside the other person. I remember a job where I wanted to finish setting the second floor joists before we left for the day. My helper, however, had decided it was time to go home. We had about 40 minutes left in the day and 24 2x12x24s to set. I thought we could do it! The way we accomplished it was for me to set the challenge, and then work right there with him to spur him on. My optimism caught on and we finished with time to spare. By setting an example of someone who is willing to hustle, you set the pace for the rest of the crew.

One-man crew. *With the one-person crew, jobs may take a little longer to complete but labor costs are kept to a minimum. Additional staff are brought onto the site only as needed.*

ADVANTAGES OF THE ONE-MAN CREW

The basic concept of the one-man crew is to run the entire job with one person on the job from start to finish, adding help only as needed, and removing help when it's no longer economically viable. This has proven to be the most efficient, productive way to manage a remodeling project. Here's why:

Improved Planning Time

Every remodeling project is different and requires planning time. There will be times on a remodeling project when the progress of the job must be stopped in order to spend time planning the next move. Anyone working there, other than the lead carpenter, needs to go to another job or his wages are being wasted. If the situation is clouded by others on the site, you can end up with either poor planning or wasted time.

Increased Efficiency

People work more efficiently by themselves. There are many good reasons for this. I don't say this as a criticism of carpenters or helpers, but as an observation of people in general.

Socializing. We are essentially social animals and will tend to talk to people with us on the job. Just as people in an office will stand around the water cooler and talk, carpenters will stand around and drink coffee and talk. When a job site opens in the morning, our natural tendency is to discuss sporting events or perhaps the events of the previous evening, and all this before the tools are unpacked.

Breaks. Breaks can run over their allotted time more easily when there are several people on the job. For safety's sake, breaks in the work day are important. These breaks can be to sit and eat a sandwich or perhaps to fill in paperwork. Whatever is done, it often consumes more time if there are more people. Consider the effect on the budget if a crew of three people overstays a break by seven minutes every day on a six-month job. The crew is costing the company $50/hour, which is $5.83 for every seven minutes, or $29.15 each week. For 26 weeks, that adds up to $757.90. There are not many of us who would want to simply give away $757.90.

Instruction time. With a one-man crew, there is no one else to explain a task to. Every carpenter has a way that he wants things to be done. If we are responsible for others on the site, it takes us time to explain why this is being done, how to do it, and, in most cases, where the materials are.

Supervision time. With a one-man crew, there is no one else to check up on. The lead carpenter is responsible for the successful completion of the job. This requires that he check people's work to ensure a high standard. This takes time. It also takes time to rework something if it is not done well.

Unnecessary help. If another person is present, it is our nature to ask for help with tasks that don't really require help. If someone else is there on the site, we may be inclined to have him help us, even if each of us could, and should, be doing separate tasks. I have watched helpers on a job hold the end of a long piece of baseboard on a miter saw instead of the carpenter taking time to set up an inanimate support. There are many ways to make tasks that are traditionally two-person jobs into one-person jobs.

Can one carpenter set kitchen cabinets? Yes! Can one carpenter install trim? Yes! Can one carpenter install siding? Yes (for most types of siding, anyway). Having two people on a task is often a big waste of manpower and therefore money.

Down time. A job can be paced more easily with a one-man crew. Given the premise that you want the lead carpenter on the job from start to finish, the question arises: What does he do while the drywall is being finished? If you have a crew on the site, they will have finished the roofing, siding, exterior trim, and the gutters before the electrical, HVAC, and plumber are done roughing in. There is nothing left to do but wait. That's very inefficient. With one carpenter working alone, the exterior work can be paced to match the interior drywall work so that his time is productively spent—while still on the site to answer questions from the subs. As soon as the drywall is finished, he can move inside to begin trim. That's very productive.

Decreased Labor Costs

A one-man crew reduces the labor cost to the job. A helper that costs the company $15/hour costs the job $600 per week to stay on the job, whether he produces anything or not. If we use him efficiently only 50% of the time, we have wasted $300 each week. If there are two jobs that can each use the helper productively 50% of his time, it still costs $600 per week, but none of that money is wasted.

Breaktime. *Several workers on the same job site often translates into greater downtime and increased needs for supervision. Efficiency declines and profits are at risk.*

Improved Client Communication

With one man on the job most of the time, there is no question of whom the homeowner should go to with questions and suggestions.

Improved Quality

The same person that laid the foundation, framed the walls, and supervised the subs is doing the trim work. He knows ahead of time where the imperfections are and has generally planned a way to deal with them. No matter how you look at it, this continuity and knowledge of the job adds up to improved quality of the work — the product you are selling to the client.

How It Works

The carpenter receives the job folder from the production manager or contractor. After he goes through the job planning process and preconstruction meetings, he is ready to physically start the work. The lead carpenter begins by working on the site by himself as long has he can. On an addition, this may be through the framing of the walls. He sees that in two days it will be time to frame the roof. A decision must be made. "Can I frame the roof by myself?" Answer: "No." (Although on some small roofs the answer may be yes.) A call is made to the person who is responsible for distributing help to the jobs. "Hi Sandi. I need a helper on the Smith job for two days. I would like him to start Monday morning at 7 a.m. and I'll need him until the end of the day Tuesday. Can you can send him to some other job on Wednesday?"

As you can see, the request must be specific. It must include the type of person you want (helper or carpenter), the day to start and the length of time you need him, and the request to send him to another job when your need for him ends. The lead carpenter then continues working on his own until another task arises that requires additional help and the process repeats.

If a job can be completed by only the lead carpenter working on the job, it will be the most efficient (meaning profitable) way to manage that job. The need will arise on many remodeling projects for more people to be working on the site. To reiterate: This should be the exception and only as needed.

OBJECTIONS TO THE ONE-MAN CREW

Talking about the one-man crew usually raises objections from both carpenters and contractors. Let's look at the most common objections and how to address them:

The homeowners won't understand why there is only one person working on the job. If the lead carpenter system is explained in advance to the clients, including how this will enhance their project, they will not mind.

It will take twice as long to complete the project. Yes, it will take longer. But just a little longer. Understanding that "more people" does not mean "faster" will help us see that the job will not take twice as long with a one-man crew. The benefits of quality control and better communication with the client will surely compensate for this issue.

It's not safe to work alone. Yes, this is a legitimate concern. And with the lead carpenter system, stronger safety standards have to be in place to prevent accidents. Precautions need to be taken to allow for emergency calls if an accident occurs. But in my experience, I haven't heard of this being an actual safety problem, but rather the fear of a safety issue.

TASK MANAGEMENT

In general, task management is the process of setting up systems to let others on the job know what has to be done and when. Here are some ways to accomplish this goal. Some stand alone; others need to be combined to be effective.

The Job Schedule

The schedule for the job should be posted for everyone to see. This allows everyone to quickly see where the job stands today and where it has to go over the following days. It also allows people to start working on the day's tasks when they might otherwise be standing around waiting for the lead carpenter to finish saying good morning to the clients.

An addendum to the job schedule is the weekly schedule. The schedule is made on Friday and breaks down the next week into daily tasks to

WEEKLY SCHEDULE

Weekly schedule for week ending: February 27, 1999

Goal: Finish framing-in prep for trades by Thursday

Steps to complete:

Monday 23	Notes	Est. Time Frame	Helpers
Roof framing	Set rafters—use 2x10x14	8 hrs	Karen and Bob

Tuesday 24			
Roof decking	Install decking; $1/2$ CDX, 5 ply	8 hrs	Karen and Bob

Wednesday 25			
Soffit framing	Misc 2x4	3 hrs	Karen
Lay out interior partitions		3 hrs	Bob
Build interior partitions	Use 2x4x8's	5 hrs	Karen and Bob

Thursday 26			
Finish interior partitions		1 hr	Karen and Bob
Back up blocking		7 hrs	Karen
Blocking for accessories		3 hrs	Bob
Calls, paperwork, administration		4 hrs	Bob

Friday 27			
Exterior trim	Use 1x6x12	8 hrs	Karen and Bob

Figure 25. *The weekly schedule, posted where everyone can see it, can save time and serve as a motivational tool.*

be accomplished. This should be detailed and understandable to anyone looking at it. It decreases the need for the lead carpenter to stop work and spend time explaining the next task to be accomplished. If the lead carpenter knows who will be on his job the next week, names can be put next to specific tasks.

These schedules should be set up with specific goals in mind tied to completing the job efficiently and profitably. The setting of goals can be a powerful motivation. Goals should challenge people's abilities but should be attainable. Each goal should have a time frame attached to it. For an example see Figure 25.

Running List of Tasks

This is a simple but effective way to manage tasks. Make your lists in a notebook that will not be thrown away. Each day move the tasks that have not been completed to the next page or next day. Add to that list any new tasks that have come up or that are on the master schedule. Include in this list calls to make, material to order, items to check, and questions to ask (Figure 26). By maintaining this running list, you will find the use of time more efficient. For example, if someone has 20 minutes to use at the end of the day, but the next big task will take three hours to complete, this running list will show you all the little things that would otherwise be ignored until later in the job, but could be done in 20 minutes.

Morning meeting. Have a meeting each morning to outline to anyone working on your site what you want to accomplish that day. Setting expectations and answering most of the questions should be the primary goal of this meeting. The meeting should be brief and to the point. Then let everyone get to work. This would be a good time to go over your list of tasks so that everyone knows what's on today's schedule.

It falls to the lead carpenter to maintain the quality dictated by his company's policies and the job specifications. This requires that he be a policeman of sorts, checking the work of others to ensure a uniform job. He should correct any mistakes and, if feasible, take time to teach the other person the proper way to handle that job. It is best to correct those items quickly — the same day if possible.

Safety

The managers of a company cannot be around each minute to check job conditions, so that responsibility falls to the lead carpenter. Having someone on site to monitor safety is one of the great benefits of the lead carpenter system. To do this, the lead needs to be educated about where and why the most common accidents occur, and how to prevent them. He must insist on safe practices on the job site at all times.

In my experience, the leading cause of serious injuries on the job are falls from scaffolds, ladders, and platforms. The next most common are from handling lumber, plywood, timbers, concrete, iron and steel (most of these accidents involve back injuries). Following these are falls from slipping or tripping on floors, stairs, working surfaces, and icy surfaces, or into excavations. Being struck by falling beams, lumber, plywood, iron, steel, and other objects, and cuts from saws (including chainsaws) and other sharp objects round out injuries on the job.

What are the major factors that contribute to these accidents, and how can these factors be lessened or eliminated?

Defective ladders, incorrect position of ladders, and overloaded ladders cause many problems. Be sure that all defective ladders are repaired or thrown away. For proper positioning, ladders should extend three feet above the landing point, such as a roof edge, should be secured tightly to the landing area, and be at a comfortable pitch. Only one person should

TASK LIST—SMITH REMODEL

AUGUST 19, 1998

Call plumber for rough in ✔

Call electrician to lay out to avoid plumber ✔

Complete back up for drywall

Work on fire stops

Check with office on handrail code requirements ✔

Install backing for bath accessories ✔

AUGUST 20, 1998

Run dryer vent

Hook up bath fan venting

Check with plumber about his close-in inspection

Install two hangers on joists in basement by furnace flue

Ask client about a time to check electrical layout

Check squeak in bath floor

AUGUST 21, 1998

Call for closein inspection

Figure 26. *A running task list, kept in a notebook on the site, is a great way to stay organized and avoid punchlist items at the end of the job.*

be on a ladder at a time. Materials and tools should not be carried up a ladder, but should be tied to a rope and hoisted up.

Improperly erected scaffolding is an injury waiting to happen. Scaffolding should be installed plumb on solid footing and secured to a solid structure. All scaffolding should have guard rails and solid walk surfaces.

Platforms without barriers are another common cause of accidents. Any landing, stair platform, or balcony more than 48" above a surface must have a railing 36" high, an intermediate rail, and a toe rail.

Slips, falls, and punctures are often caused by a dirty and disorganized job site, slippery shoes, inadequate lighting, and exposed nails. To maintain a safe job, keep the site clean and organized on a daily basis, which helps with efficiency as well. Wear slip-resistant shoes and require other employees on the job to do so. Be sure all work areas are sufficiently lighted.

Unprotected ends of reinforcing rods can cause injuries. All ends of reinforcing rods must have approved protection. And all exposed nails should be pulled or bent over. Nails driven to hold tools should be at a height above contact by most people.

Falling objects hurt many workers on job sites. The best advice is to avoid working under other work that's above you or under a suspended object. If necessary, wear a hard hat and require other employees to do so. Make sure all materials are stacked securely and safely.

Cuts and eye problems happen all too often in our line of work. Be sure to train workers sufficiently in saw operation. Be sure there is a way to lock out power during blade changing. Install safety guards on all equipment and require employees to use push sticks. Make the use of eye protection in certain circumstances a requirement of employment.

Lifting injuries can ruin a worker for a day or a lifetime. Give employees sufficient training on lifting techniques. Use mechanical lifts whenever possible; these can be rented very inexpensively. Use enough people to lift any object. When working in a one-man crew, plan ahead to carry heavy objects when others are there to help. To carry heavy objects over rough terrain, clear a path of travel before lifting and moving the object.

There are many reasons and excuses for not being safe on the job site. These come from all parts of the company. They range from "I've been doin' it this way for 20 years and I ain't been hurt yet" to "We can't afford a new ladder right now so just use that one." No matter where these reasons and excuses come from, the lead carpenter must insist that his job is safe. There are good publications out that can give more details on the subject.

WORKING WITH PEOPLE

Even when operating as a one-man crew, the lead carpenter never works in a vacuum, and must learn how to work with others if the job is to be a success. Starting with the company owner and working our way through the clients, subs, inspectors, and other employees, we will explore the practical aspects of dealing with all the people who impact the job.

However you approach getting people to work with you to complete a job will often determine the success or failure of the job. Whether it is your boss, clients, subs, or other employees, how you treat them will enhance their work or hinder it. We often hear excuses about how the job went sour because of what others did or didn't do, but a careful study will show us that many problems could have been avoided through good "people skills."

Dealing With the Boss

In remodeling, the boss is generally the principal of the company. Bosses are sometimes the hardest people to get along with. But there are good reasons for that. They often work too many hours and are tired. It is not unusual for the principal of a remodeling company to work 60 to 80 hours a week. Many wonder why they do it. Others are what I call "control freaks." They have worked for other people but went into business for themselves, in part, because they want the control of the company in their hands. They believe they know the right way to run a company. Many haven't worked in the field for a while, and have inflated ideas about what can be done in a day. Even I have done this as a production manager. Because I don't have to do the work everyday, it is sometimes hard for me to see what can and can't be done in a given amount of time.

Bosses have their lives tied up in this business. For the carpenter, it is often just a job, but for the principal in the company it is sometimes his entire lifestyle. He often has money tied up in the venture, he has emotional capital, he has time tied up, and he has his retirement invested in the company.

So, given this mindset of the contractor, what is the best way to work with him or her? Do the best work you can. Contractors respect people who work hard and fairly. Don't worry about doing it right all the time. Bosses recognize their own faults and will accept some of yours. Recognizing that they have so much tied up in this business lets them know that you understand and want the company to succeed as well. Give the company a full day. Be positive — no griping or complaining.

Recognize that the boss will do anything that is needed to make the company succeed and that he respects those who will do the same. If a footer has to be dug by hand, do it willingly. If the toilet has to be cleaned, do it willingly. If something should be changed in the company, make the suggestion in a positive, helpful way. Constructive criticism will show a willingness to work together and an interest in helping the company to succeed.

Register any complaints directly with the boss. Gossip and rumor will destroy the morale of the company and can mean the difference between a profit and loss. If you hear rumors about personnel problems, client problems, carpenters that are bad-mouthing the company, all that should go directly to the boss. Work as a team member. This is not an adversarial relationship, but a cooperative one. The contractor needs you and you need him. Any principal in a company realizes that the people he employs are his main asset. Most employers are interested in improving the company and are open to working with the employees to see it happen. The division between management and the field must be dissolved by open and trusting dialogue.

Finally, if you can't work in a company, leave. We must realize that, to some degree, no matter how good a boss is, there will be some things that will not change. If we cannot accept the way the boss runs the company, we are better off in a different company, and the boss is better off without us.

Managing Clients

Have you ever noticed that very few stories are told about the "clients from heaven" but lots are told about the "clients from hell"? This is not because those clients don't exist but it is because our brains are wired to remember bad more easily than to remember good. I've heard that it takes ten good experiences to offset one bad experience. What we fail to remember is that our clients have an experience with us also and what they share with their friends and neighbors will often determine where our next job comes from, or doesn't! So we must learn how to work with clients instead of against them, for their good as well as ours.

Getting along with clients is sometimes very easy and sometimes can be the most challenging part of the job. There are four basic ideas that we ought to understand about most of our clients:

1) Clients want a good experience. Even more important than the finished product is the way it is done.

2) They want to feel good about the amount of money they are spending to change their living space.

3) They want to know they are doing the right thing.

4) Our clients are usually more than one person. Husbands and wives, brothers and sisters, roommates, etc., don't always see the project from the same perspective.

Sometimes anger directed at a carpenter is the result of a disagreement between the partners in the home. The lead carpenter will likely become the arbitrator of several disputes during the course of a job. One of the partners is usually more dominant than the other. One is usually the main decision maker. Knowing which is which will make a difference in the way the job is run.

Usually, clients don't know as much about design or construction as they think they do. Our clients are more educated than ever by reading articles and talking with friends, but they are not the professionals. Knowing this will help us to realize that although clients can talk about the project, they may not fully understand the issues they are discussing. They usually cannot visualize the completed project. Even people that work with blueprints everyday have trouble visualizing what the finished project will look like. Knowing this can help the lead carpenter better understand the client's perspective.

With these things in mind, what can you do to get along with your clients?

Maintain a positive attitude. Even when all seems to be going downhill and people are yelling, always find something good about the situation. Every job will have difficulties and problems, but focusing on them will only cause the client to focus on them as well, which will further deteriorate their comfort level. Emphasize positive aspects of the job. Comments like, "This room will be beautiful" and "You have really created a nice space here" will reinforce their decision to do this project. Even when your client is angry or upset, your attitude will rub off on them and help maintain a good atmosphere.

Speak directly to your clients. Our tendency will be to hope that the clients don't speak to us. We often feel the tension of the client/company relationship. Or perhaps you are just the kind of person who would rather work than talk. Find out early on in the project how the clients would like to be addressed, Mr., Mrs., Tom, Sue. Look them in the eye, showing respect for yourself and them. Find reasons to get their input. Involve them in the process of building.

Practice "show and tell." Instead of just talking about ideas you have, draw out your ideas and details so the clients can see what you're talking about. Walk through the job with them and show them the work that's been done. Give them an idea of how the work will continue. This will require time, but will save time in the long run by catching errors and changes before they become big problems. Show you care about what they tell you and validate it by writing down all their input. Carry a pad and paper while you are talking with a client. It is a good idea to have a form where you can record these meetings for future reference. Use common language that they can understand. This will take work, but it's worth it.

Provide a place and system for communicating. A communication center gives the client a sense of staying in touch with the construction process. They can leave you notes and you can provide information or questions for them. Keep them informed about the schedule.

Keep the clients informed about job progress. This will give them a sense that they are still in control of the project. You have to know your subcontractors and suppliers so that the information you give clients is correct, but it is critical that the clients be well informed.

An important part of this is learning how to listen effectively to the clients. This means listening to *how* they say something in addition to *what* they say. Begin early to "read" your client's true feelings and intentions so that you can understand them better. Never believe it if they say "this is a minor point." If a client brings something to your attention, respond to his or her ideas and requests quickly even if it does seem like a minor thing.

Working With Inspectors

There are still some areas of the country that do not have any code enforcement, but by and large we are governed by building codes and the people that enforce them. To relate effectively with inspectors, it helps to understand what their role is in the building process. If you ask a builder this question, he might say, "to be a pain in the neck." If you ask a home-owner, she will say, "I don't know." However, if you ask a building inspector what his primary role is, he's likely to say "consumer protection." There have been so many incidents of poor building standards, hazardous practices, and rip-off schemes, consumers need some type of safeguard against these problems.

So the codes were written and the inspectors were put in place. The next logical question is: What is their liability in this area? The answer is, as it turns out, virtually none. If an inspector sees an infraction and does not report it, there is a small chance he will be held liable. But if an inspector does not see an infraction and a problem develops, there is no liability. So what we have is an individual with final authority in terms of building codes, but no liability.

One implication of this is that passing an inspection in no way guarantees that the building is correctly built or safe, and does not get your company off the hook for liability. Another is that inspectors can make your life easy or miserable with few risks to themselves.

The fact is that how you relate to and treat an inspector will determine how a job progresses, as well as its profitability. Here are some suggestions on working with inspectors to make a job go smoother:

Get a name if possible. Everyone likes to be addressed by his name. Inspectors are no different. It shows respect and an interest in him as a person and not as an adversary. Find out his interests and be ready to talk hunting, fishing, golf, or whatever.

Check your work carefully. Get a reputation for having your work ready and up to code. If an inspector has reason to believe that you are not going to try to slide anything past him, he will work more efficiently with you. What you want is an inspector who will check your work but will not feel it necessary to look at every little piece.

Ask questions about future potential problems. If there are areas of work coming up that you are not sure of, take time to ask about them while he is there on the job. This gives you an opportunity to find out from the person who will be inspecting the work what he will want, and helps him to gain a sense of trust regarding your standards, not distrust. It also gives you an opportunity to find out about changes to the code that are pending and how they may affect you.

Know your local procedures and codes. It is important that you know what you must do and show that knowledge to the inspector. It is also important that if you are in a situation where the inspector is wrong or there is vagueness to the code, that you know where to call to get approval or clarification.

Working with inspectors is important because a failed inspection will affect the flow of any job. It will affect the subcontractors and throw off their schedules. It will cause you to change course in mid-stream and perhaps do work out of sequence. Or perhaps it will cause a total shut down so that you are out of work or forced to go to a different job temporarily. Failing an inspection is demoralizing and can affect the feelings and attitudes of everyone on the job.

Working With Architects

Much like inspectors, architects have a reputation for having lots of influence but little accountability. Unless we understand architects and work with them, there can be problems. In defense of architects, the contribution they make to a project can, and often does, mean the difference between a nice project and a great project. You should understand these truths about architects:

Architects are often more concerned about form and beauty than costs. This automatically sets up a conflict with the builder, who is trying to control cost so that he can make a profit. The architect wants to produce a beautiful project that will not only please the client, but also please himself and perhaps win an award. Architects' lives and livelihoods are often deeply tied up in their work.

Like principals in a company, architects are emotionally involved in their work. A project is not just a house, but an artistic creation. Slights to the design are slights against them. Disregard for a detail may be perceived as a snub to their egos. More importantly, the appearance of the finished product is what brings them more work. They design with the end result in mind, not necessarily understanding how it can be achieved. They are concerned not with the process, but with the results. The reputation of an architect is based on a look that he develops and his future work is dependent on that look being realized. Some architects do not respect the abilities of the carpenters that produce the work. This attitude has been fostered over many years by carpenters and builders that do not care enough about detail, who will let anything slide, but most of all, by carpenters who won't try anything new.

Here is how to deal more effectively with architects:

Find out their involvement level. Before you start the project, find out in detail how involved the client wants the architect to be. An architect's involvement can be as detached as preparation of the plans only, as involved as daily site inspection, or anything in between. Once you know the answer, you can adjust your expectations about how much contact you will have with the architect and how much influence he will have on the day-to-day operations.

Know the plans. It is important when working with an architect to know the plans completely and be able to justify what you've done. Remember, you must win his respect by showing your ability to read, understand, and implement his ideas. In discussions with him, show that you've looked ahead and seen how the roof will tie into the trim details. He will appreciate your involvement and even your suggestions if they are made tactfully and help translate his design ideas into a real building.

Since the architect is involved in the project, it is important to "work the plans" and not change them. This shows respect for his ability to create. As your contract with the client allows, consult with the architect about what he wants to achieve, how the look is developing, and address any questions about how it is progressing.

Successfully Managing Subs

Managing the subcontractors on a job can be a challenge. Carpenters often speak about having to babysit subs, and it may seem that way to us. But the way we manage their work will often dictate how they perform for us.

It is important for the lead carpenter to know the scope of work required of each subcontractor. This is necessary so that he can ensure that all of the work is completed according to specifications. The scope of work is dictated by the contract the company has with the sub. This contract must be in writing, contain enough information so that an individual other than the salesman can understand it, and must be given to the lead.

The lead must also know the job specs as they relate to that sub. The lead is the last person to check and make sure the two contracts agree. If they don't, the lead must bring it to someone's attention to find out how to proceed. Armed with the contract and the specifications, the lead can then insist that they be followed. Many jobs have turned sour over a subcontractor either cutting a corner or just doing a job the best way he knew how, but not following the specs.

Sometimes the specs don't make sense, sometimes they simply can't be done as described, and sometimes it is just plain harder to do it that way. But the specs must be followed. If a spec can't be followed because of existing conditions or is simply impossible, the lead can make a call to resolve the matter.

When installation is finished, the lead is responsible for checking the work for completeness. This inspection is best done off a checklist to be sure nothing is missed (Figure 27). One missed outlet in a tile backsplash can cost large sums of money if it is not caught until the final inspection. If the plumber forgets to glue a joint or solder a pipe, it can cost large sums of money once the water is finally turned on. A missed detail on a brick foundation can cost plenty unless it is fixed at an early stage.

Technical knowledge. The lead carpenter does not need to know all the codes for each sub's trade, but should be generally familiar with them. He needs to know enough about the code to catch work that will not pass inspection or is simply dangerous. He also needs enough knowledge to be ready for the sub. For instance, a toilet rough-in is standard at $12\frac{1}{2}$ inches off the back wall and at least $15\frac{1}{2}$ inches from a side wall. We all know this, but how many times is a plumber asked to cut out a joist because it is in the way? Not only have we wasted his time but we have wasted ours as well. We also have added one more notch to our gun that says "plumbers are always cutting out joists and just leaving them,"

```
┌─────────────────────────────────────────────────────────────┐
│              SUBTRADE INSPECTION SIGN-OFF SHEET               │
│                                                               │
│  ELECTRICAL ROUGH IN                                          │
│                                                               │
│  Receptacles to code _____✔_____                            │
│                                                               │
│  Switches and lights per walk through plans _____✔_____     │
│                                                               │
│  Smoke detectors in each bedroom _____✔_____                │
│                                                               │
│  Receptacle placement in kitchen _____✔_____                │
│                                                               │
│  Receptacle and switch placement with respect to furniture placement___✔_____ │
│                                                               │
│  Door swing and switches _____✔_____                        │
│                                                               │
│  TPF panel inspection _____✔_____                           │
│                                                               │
│  Door bell installed _____✔_____                            │
│                                                               │
│  Phones roughed in _____✔_____                              │
│                                                               │
│  TV wires roughed in _____✔_____                            │
│                                                               │
│  Security roughed in _____✔_____                            │
│                                                               │
│                                                               │
│                                                               │
│  Rough in complete                                            │
│                                                               │
│                                                               │
│  Larry Lead                                                   │
│  ──────────────────────────────────                          │
│  Site Superintendent                                          │
└─────────────────────────────────────────────────────────────┘
```

Figure 27. *A checklist or sign-off sheet, such as this one, can help the lead be sure a subcontractor's work is complete, saving time and money for the company.*

when in reality we are at fault. In the case of working with subs, a little knowledge is a good thing.

Working relationship. As I mentioned earlier, a subcontractor's behavior can be heavily influenced by what we do and how we treat him. In general, if we treat him considerately, we will receive the same treatment back. Adopt a positive approach. Do not refer to this part of the job as babysitting. Think about what that implies about the sub. This is not adversarial. This is a team effort. Use first names or nicknames. "Hey Sparky" is not a good way to develop a team spirit (unless his nickname is Sparky!).

Communicate your expectations early. Meet the sub at the door. Explain what the "house rules" are. (No smoking, radios, etc.) Explain what you want to accomplish that day. Remember that sometimes subcontractors send employees out without enough information to do their job. Don't take it out on them. If this happens, walk them through so they can do their job. Remember, you want them to complete their work so you can stay on schedule. Be cooperative. If the sub needs some framing done, help out. If he needs to carry a tub, help out. If he needs a tool (you can draw the line at a sub's tools!), help out.

Scheduling Subcontractors

We have all had trouble with subs who don't show up when they are supposed to. We must understand that, unlike a carpenter on a job, subs have many places calling for their attention. Often these calls conflict and run over schedule, making it hard to predict when they will be available. But the actions of an organized, diligent lead carpenter can make the system work much better. Here are a few tips I have found helpful:

Use your job schedule to notify the sub as far ahead as possible about when you will need him. A month is great if you have a job that runs that long.

Give him a call one week ahead to remind and bring him up-to-date on your schedule. This is critical because he will know a little more about his schedule at this time, and your schedule will be more definitively set as well. During that phone call, give the sub all the details that you can about what you want done. If you want the electrician for rough in, give him model numbers for the recessed lights, the number of appliances, exactly what areas you want him to work in, etc. Also, tell him if there are any changes to the plan as he bid it.

Ask for, or even require, a site visit between the call and beginning the work. This will help avoid the sub coming to the job and walking off because he didn't bring the right materials.

Confirm the appointment with the sub two days before and include a discussion about the time of arrival. This is often a serious point of contention. "First thing" means different things to different people. For someone to say "I'll be there on Thursday" could mean that he will show up on Thursday at 3:30 p.m. and talk to the carpenter about what will happen on Friday.

Confirm the date, the time, and scope of work 24 hours ahead. You cannot call a sub too much, even if you are just leaving messages on an answering machine.

Once the sub arrives, allow him to work without interference. Remember there is some other carpenter waiting for him on another job. ◪

Chapter 10

Post-Job Responsibilities

It is the lead carpenter's responsibility to follow through on all work on the site, down to the final nail or piece of trim. However, the work does not stop there. The lead has invested too many hours in the project to simply throw away all that he has learned. The lead should be used in three important ways after the job is complete. The first is to help evaluate the estimate and provide feedback to the sales crew. The second is to make warranty calls. The third is education.

ESTIMATE EVALUATION AND FEEDBACK

The first post-job responsibility is to evaluate the estimate and provide feedback to the salesperson. For years and years, our carpenters have been asking for the opportunity to review the estimates of jobs before they are sold. After working with a few, or many, estimates that are way off the mark, carpenters naturally assume that they could have foreseen all the problems, and therefore could have helped craft a better estimate. For contractors, however, such a system is not practical. There is only so much that you can have the lead do. In addition, the carpenters are benefiting from 20-20 hindsight. Neither they, nor the estimator can see all the ramifications of a job as well at the beginning as they can at the end.

So estimators, as well as carpenters, learn from experience what works and what doesn't, as well as what the company can accomplish in a certain amount of time. The thing to do is use the hindsight of all involved to increase the accuracy of future estimates. One way to accomplish this is to have the carpenter give feedback to the estimators on the accuracy of the estimate as part of the post-job evaluation. How does the estimate compare to real life? This can be done in a one-hour meeting on the site

"The lead carpenters have the nitty gritty on the project. This helps to close out the job, because things are handled as they come up. It cuts down the incredibly large list that seems to grow at the end of the job if somebody's not taking care of it."

JOHN McGOWAN
Production Manager
Sass Construction, Inc.
Excelsior, Minnesota

or in the office. This step in the process can be a real winner for everyone. It builds teamwork between the estimators and the field crews. They begin to feel that they are working together, not as adversaries. They start to understand how each other operates. They start to understand why others do their job the way they do. This step also provides the estimator with valuable information on the real costs of doing the work, both increases and decreases.

For many years we were finding out that our framing budgets were not being met but our window installation budgets were always more than ample. The temptation, of course, was to blame the carpenters for not working hard enough on framing and to trim the window budget. This would trim the contract price and allow us to sell more work because the clients were shopping us against the competition on price.

In conversations with the carpenters, we found out that they were spending a lot of time with subs during the framing stage of the work. All this was being coded to the framing stage and therefore sending the budget out of line. This prompted the bosses of the company to create a new line item in the estimate to budget money for supervision of subcontractors. We also took some of the money that we had in window installation and allocated it to framing, and continued to help the carpenters improve their framing skills. The knowledge of the budget that accumulates over the course of the job should be used to its full advantage at the end by sharing it with everyone.

MAKING WARRANTY CALLS

Warranty items will occur on all jobs within the first year of completion. I recommend that all companies have proactive warranty programs. In other words, tell the clients that you will call them in three, six, and nine months to walk through and look for items that were missed in the punchlist or simply need a little attention. This will put your clients at ease that you are not taking the money and running.

The lead carpenter is the ideal person to follow up on warranty calls. The reasons for this are simple. First, he has the relationship to assure the client that the follow-up work will be done properly. The client and the lead often develop a strong relationship based on trust that is built over the course of three to six months of "living together." The clients will often recommend the lead by name to friends. The fact that there are callbacks can be disturbing to some clients, but the trust that has been built with the lead can often mitigate those negative feelings.

Plus, the lead knows the project like nobody else. Trying to explain to a newcomer on the job where or what something is can be time-consuming. The lead can understand the items on a warranty list very easily. It requires very little explanation, and, therefore, little time to explain to the lead where the trim is loose or which cabinet door is out of line. He is familiar with the work. It may even be a good idea to arrange for the lead to make the warranty inspection. In this way, he can see the work that has to be done first hand and can often rectify every problem the same day. On many occasions the lead may still have a little bit of trim or caulk left from the job, or may know where it was stored, so that no more money has to be spent for those little items. All of this requires that the lead be able to spend some time with this follow-up. These small jobs become ideal fillers for rain days on the new job or days when the lead can get the subs working and leave them for a few hours. He can do the warranty work on the prior job and return at the end of the day to lock up the current job.

EDUCATION

The third use of the leads at the end of the job should be education. This has already occurred with the sales staff by evaluating the estimate. The lead can now share something he learned on the job with others in the company. I remember a situation when I was still working in the field. I had to cut into a slate roof, remove the slate and salvage it, and create a dormer. I did this from the inside by cutting out the roof deck in a small area from underneath and creating a small hole at first. I worked from there out until I had room to nail in toe boards and create a safe work area. This also protected the roof from rain until I was ready to demo and build the dormer. About the same time, another lead was working on a project that was similar to mine. The production manager had him call me for an explanation of how I did it so that he could take the same approach. In this case, the education took place during the job, but these kinds of new techniques picked up on the job can translate into valuable learning tools for everyone in the company. ◪

Chapter 11

Frequently Asked Questions

If the lead carpenter is spending time ordering, answering questions, and filling out paperwork, when does he have time to do production?

That's an excellent question. Time spent in production will vary depending on the amount of paperwork required by individual companies, and the size and complexity of each job. I will address each of these issues.

1) Every company should evaluate how much paperwork it wants a lead carpenter to fill out. The paperwork should be kept to a minimum so the lead has adequate time to produce the product. Also consider who in the company is best qualified to fill in the paperwork, who can get it most accurate, and what you are willing to pay to get the paperwork done. From my perspective, the person most qualified to accurately process job-site paperwork is the lead carpenter. In this way, it is not a waste of time, but a profitable use of time. The idea that paperwork is a waste of time has to be discarded by the contractor and the lead when this system is implemented.

2) The size of the job will affect the time spent in production. Large jobs will require more management time. When a job reaches a volume of $400,000 to $500,000, the lead really becomes a project manager and cannot do any significant amount of production on the site. It may be better to simply have a site manager who does not do production in those cases. Most companies around the country that use lead carpenters fall into a smaller-volume range. A survey I conducted at several of my seminars indicated that the majority of leads in all sections of the country spend between 10% and 20% of

their time in management and the rest in production. Bear in mind that this includes all of the management, not just the paperwork. Therefore, the paperwork doesn't need to, and shouldn't, take very much time. (For more, see Chapter 8.)

How do you deal with the lead carpenter having nothing to do after the subs come in?

Remember, I am a strong proponent of the one-man crew. If the job or task can be done by one person, it should be. With this in mind, the contractor needs to train the leads to plan the work so they remain productive. This may mean saving the siding or roofing work until the subs are inside the addition. It may mean doing some of the work themselves that would normally be done by subs. It may mean doing some work out of sequence. In some cases, we start setting doors and running trim while the drywall finisher is still blocking and skimming. This is not the ideal, but it is better than not working. The trick is to plan the work to avoid idle time.

If the work cannot be run this way, it is a good idea to save warranty work from previous jobs or perhaps keep a running list of all the little jobs your clients have asked you to do but you haven't had a free carpenter for. This can work as a kind of client handyman service that helps fill in these gaps in your larger jobs. Even so, it's important for the lead to check in with the subs and/or clients on his current job at the beginning of the day and again at the end of the day to keep some continuity. (For more, see Chapter 9.)

What do you look for more in hiring, good people skills or good carpentry skills?

Both skills are critical for the role of lead carpenter. In looking to fill a job, I would look for both and interview with both in mind. If you have to settle for one over the other, however, go for the good people skills and good management skills and then train your lead in carpentry. (Of course, he has to have at least a working knowledge of carpentry and some craft skills.) If you have to hire a novice carpenter, try to hire at least six months before you need to use him in a lead position so he can pick up some trade skills by working with another lead. (See Chapter 5.)

In your company, do you have fixed crews or do people float?

In the lead carpenter system, there are no crews. The leads are the crews, and the helpers, second carpenters, and laborers float among them as needed. This call is made by the lead, with coordination help from the contractor or other office staff. If the company is big enough, this is typically the production manager. Hopkins and Porter has operated this way for years. (See Chapter 9.)

How aware is the lead carpenter of the budget?

I believe that the lead carpenter should be fully aware of the budget for the job he is doing. In this system, you are asking the lead to manage the job to make a profit. He can't do that if he doesn't know where costs stop and profit begins.

For example, if a lead is ordering material, say trim for a fascia, he will often order what he needs, plus some, just in case. Properly trained, however, a lead will consult his budget and probably see that there is not enough money to order the "plus some." He will order more precisely and use every piece. Or if he is planning the framing, he can look at the budget and see if it will allow for a third man or if he can make do with two until the need for a third man is really critical.

If you do not make the lead aware of the budget, then someone else must be making all those calls, and that will cost you time and money. Be aware, however, that you cannot simply hand the lead the budget and expect him to use it well. In fact, if you simply hand it to him, it will probably come around and bite you. Training the lead to think in terms of the budget is an ongoing process and a critical step in this system.

Where do you find good lead carpenters?

There are several tactics to attracting good people. Here are a few:

1) Become known in the community as a company that takes care of its employees. The good carpenters will want to work for a good company.

2) Look among contractors who have grown tired of working both ends of the company and simply want to build projects.

3) Don't hire for a lead, but hire helpers that will make good leads in the future. Then spend time training them to work your way. This is often the best approach. Unfortunately this requires long-range planning, which is hard for many people in this business.

4) Ask your current employees for suggestions of who to contact. Ask them to let you know if they meet someone who would make a good employee. Let it be known that you are constantly taking applications for future job openings. (See Chapter 5.)

 How do you protect yourself from lead carpenters who leave the company and take your clients and business leads?

 The fact is that workers in this business tend to move around a lot, and it's possible that one of your lead carpenters will someday become a competitor. Still, the important question to ask is not, "How do I protect myself?" but, "Is this employee more valuable to me trained or left in the dark?" I believe you are better off training him and giving him a good reason to stay—such as a positive company culture and fair compensation. Then hope for the best. Some companies have their employees sign non-compete clauses when they hire them. These are typically in force during employment and for a year after. We do not do this and I recommend consultation with a lawyer before you do take this step.

 Do you give the lead carpenters the power to hire and fire?

 No, we do not. This is a role best reserved for the principal of a company. There are too many personalities involved for this to be fairly handled by a lead. I do know that some companies will hire a lead on a provisional basis and send him to work with another lead for a month. The feedback from that lead will influence the permanent placement of the new hire. This seems like a good idea if a company can work it into the system. In terms of firing, this must be done carefully and systematically. Any negative information that comes in from a lead should be filed and used in the future as needed, but the ultimate decision to fire should be left to the contractor.

Q: What do you give the lead carpenters as an incentive? Do you give them a percentage of what they save over the budget?

 A: I am in favor of bonuses and incentives if they work to effectively motivate the employees. Some people are motivated by extra money. Some are motivated by threats (although these people generally don't make good leads!). Some are motivated by recognition. Some by being involved in decision-making. I suggest that you talk with the leads in your company and arrive at a plan that they will buy into. (See Chapter 5.)

....

 Q: If your volume has been growing and you have three lead carpenters and all of a sudden your volume drops sharply, what do you do? Keep your lead carpenters and lay off your regular carpenters?

 A: There are two issues involved here. The first is to try and control your volume through good business planning. It is not the purpose of this book to explain how to do that, but other books, training sessions, and peer groups can give you guidance.

The second issue is who to let go first. This is a decision that must be made carefully and deliberately. I believe that the leads are going to be your most productive employees in the long run and you should try to keep them on. Hopkins and Porter went through a slow period in the winter of '97-'98. A decision was made to keep the company working at a great cost to our bottom line. In other words, we kept the employees busy but not productively, at least not in terms of profit. This was a decision made by the principals for that time. It could easily be a different decision next time.

As business gets slow, it is a good idea to let the employees know so that they can plan. Perhaps they can plan for a short vacation or plan to do a little side work to carry them through. They can plan to look for other work if necessary.

Another approach that has helped us is to "rent out" a carpenter to a company with whom we have a friendly relationship. This keeps the carpenter busy and helps out the other contractor who may need someone for a short period of time.

Q: At my company, we're just getting ready to slowly start working into this process. How do I get my existing clients to start deferring to the lead carpenter instead of relating exclusively to me?

A: The preconstruction conference is the key to "passing the baton" of command. It is a good idea to allow the lead, once trained, to run the preconstruction conference. At the meeting, the salesman tells the client that this is the time that he is turning over the project to the production department and that from now on the lead carpenter is the one that the client should go to with questions. He then turns the meeting over to production. In our case, there is both a production manager and a lead carpenter. In most companies, it will be just the lead carpenter. Although it is important for the contractor to step way back at this point, it is equally important that he let the client know he is still available if really needed.

The next step is to not allow the client to draw you—the contractor or salesperson—back in. It's likely that, even after the baton-passing meeting, the clients will call you. Be sure you stay involved, but turn the questions back to the lead when it is his domain. For example, if a client calls and wants to know about why Clause E in the contract is so vague, that is the contractor's domain. He should answer the question. If the client calls and wants to know about the schedule, or why a wall was moved a little, that is the lead's domain. By simply saying "Have you asked Bob about that?" you can defer back to the lead very easily. It will only take a few times before the clients turn to the lead for all these types of questions.

Inevitably, you will encounter clients who will not allow you to step out. Handle this tactfully but come to an agreement, in writing if necessary, about what each person's role will be (see Chapter 8).

Q: I know I need to switch to the lead carpenter system in order to grow and maintain quality. But I'm pretty sure that none of my four carpenters want to have that much responsibility. Do I need to start over and hire all new people?

A: This is something I've seen happen. The transition to the lead carpenter system can be complicated if you have employees already on board who balk at the idea of change. There are several things that can be done in this situation:

First, be sure you clearly outline what you expect a lead carpenter to do, and then properly train the individuals to help them move into the lead position. Point out that, in many cases, the workload will not change substantially at first. Rather, there will be a gradual increase in work load and even then it will not be oppressive. For instance, the paperwork seems to be an overwhelming thing for many potential lead carpenters. Even in this book, there appears to be a lot of paperwork to do. But if you actually sit down and do the paperwork each day, you will find that it takes no more than 10 to 15 minutes per day. In other words, help the leads understand in real terms how this will affect their day.

Second, determine if one of the carpenters wants to try out the lead role for a while. Pick the carpenter who seems most interested, and ask if he will give it a try. If it works for him, he may be able to influence another to join in.

Third, hire a new person to be a lead and use the others as second carpenters. They will either stay right where they are (content to limit their earnings), leave to look for work elsewhere, or see the benefits and join in. In either case, you are winning. In all cases, though, the change should be gradual.

 All my carpenters are young. I think they could be good lead carpenters, but I'm afraid my clients will not see the leads as authority figures and continue to want to talk with me or the production manager. What advice can you give?

 This can be a problem, particularly if the company is established — and you have a reputation for being on the job yourself and your clients tend to turn to you because of that. To turn this around, you must encourage everyone to think of the lead carpenter as a person with authority. This all starts at the point of initial contact with the salesperson. In the first few visits, the clients need to be brought on board with the idea that there will be a lead carpenter who runs their job. This is why it is important that all members of the company buy into the system. The process then carries over to the preconstruction meeting. If the salesperson turns the meeting over to the lead carpenter and allows the lead to run the meeting, it will instill confidence in the client that the carpenter knows what he is doing and that the salesperson trusts the lead carpenter. It is also important for the contractor/salesperson to say the words — that he trusts the lead. Just like saying "I love you" to a spouse on a regular basis, it builds trust and confidence. If a lead is young looking, a brief history of what he has done for the company will help. Perhaps some pictures of the projects he has completed. And as the job progresses, speaking regularly to the client about the quality of the lead's work helps increase the trust. And if clients trust the lead carpenter, they tend to be much less reactive when little or big things don't go according to plan.

I find that my lead carpenters give away too much work when they get too friendly with the customer. It almost seems better for them not to have friendly contact with the customer. How would you address this problem?

The best way to curb this tendency is through education and reward. The leads must be educated about the way the company makes money and what the real profit margins of the company are. When I was working in the field, I saw paperwork that led me to believe that the company was making large quantities of money. So what is a little free work for the client? How can it hurt? What I learned later was that the company was making money but not nearly in such large quantities. This needs to be addressed on a job-by-job basis and on a yearly basis. A specific job may make a good profit for the company. But what about the whole year? Many companies only realize a 3-5% net profit, so each little "gift" to the client becomes important.

You can also curb this tendency by rewarding the lead carpenter. Look carefully to see how to tie bonuses and pay increases to the profits of a job. Consider the items that the lead controls, keeping in mind that there are others who contribute to the success or failure of the job, and see if you can help your lead to remember not to give anything away. Finally, keep your eyes open. Look at the job regularly to see if work is being done that doesn't have an accompanying paper trail. If the tendency to give away work persists, then termination of the lead, or relieving him of lead status, is in order.

The term "lead carpenter" doesn't sound like a position with a lot of authority. It almost sounds like he's just in charge of other carpenters. What do you think about calling that person a project manager, project superintendent, or a lead man?

I believe any term that works for your company and clients is fine. I do believe, however, that a gender-neutral term is better than lead man. Although in this book I have chosen to refer to the lead as "he" (for ease of reading), I recognize that some of the best leads are women, and contractors around the country should be cultivating that labor source. A company that uses gender-neutral titles will be better able to attract women into the company.

 In our company, we have constant complaints from the leads that the salesman sold the job too cheap, and from the salesman that the leads do not bring the jobs in on budget because of sloppy supervising. How can I stop this constant war?

 You have several options. But first, let me say that I believe the nature of the system will always generate a little tension. The trick is to make it as little as possible and as friendly as possible. Your best ally in keeping this conflict to a dull roar is to educate those involved. The leads need some idea of what it takes for a salesperson to actually sell a job. They need to see the process so they can see that salespeople are trying to sell the job for as much as they can, but in many cases are dealing with highly educated customers who know how to negotiate. At the same time, the salespeople need to see what goes on in the field. They need an education about how long it takes to perform certain tasks. They need to know what it is like to work daily in someone's home.

This education needs to be done on a regular basis in two-way dialogue. You can provide opportunities for the field to inform the sales staff on the budgets, the process of the job, and on details that work in the field and the details that are economical to build. Give the sales staff opportunities to inform the field about complaints that clients give them, about ways that they believe jobs could be run better. But perhaps the best solution is to develop a team and a team-oriented approach. It has to be understood by all that the running of a company requires everyone to work together. We need each other for the company to succeed, so instead of complaining, which is the norm, the standard must become constructive criticism with the goal of improving the company.

How do I know when to move a lead carpenter onto the next job? On the one hand, there's always pickup work that the lead knows all about. On the other hand, I'd rather have him starting another job and having a less skilled person do the pickup work. How does your company handle this?

In theory, the lead carpenter should stay until every little detail is resolved and the client is 100% satisfied. In practice, this rarely happens. Here are some scenarios that demonstrate when it may be a good idea to move the lead before the end of the job (each has its advantages, as well as its downside):

1) All the remaining details are items for subs to complete. Perhaps this is installation of a dishwasher that has been back-ordered. Or a paint touch-up list to complete. Or perhaps several items of this type on a list.

2) The next job requires all of the lead's time, not just a part of the day. We try to get the lead to start planning the next job while he is finishing the details on the first. A good example in my company is a lead who is finishing a kitchen redo, as this book is being written, and who will be given another job to start work on in a week. This will allow him some planning time on the second job as he is winding down the first.

3) There is another competent lead available who can finish up the details. I believe this will cost you the transfer of information, etc., but it may be worth it.

4) If you have a carpenter or helper on your staff who is used to following behind the leads to finish up, you can probably have him do this and still make money. Our company has developed a Job Completion Policy to help with this very problem. The lead starts finishing the job at least three weeks before he really thinks he will be done. This involves working with the client to develop lists each week of this three-week period. This allows the carpenter to address all the clients' concerns before the final day. This policy is helping us to better meet the goal of ending a job cleanly. ◪

Chapter 12

Four Case Studies

*T*HE KEY THING ABOUT THE LEAD CARPENTER SYSTEM, WHICH *I* HOPE *I*'VE CONVEYED to both the contractors and carpenters who will read this book, is that it is an ideal concept that can be applied in each company a little differently, depending on the individual company's needs and style. The one constant among companies that employ the system is that they utilize an employee who swings a hammer to perform job-site management of some sort as well.

As I've said in other chapters, the lead carpenter system is a process and should evolve as the company evolves and as the need for changes in management arises. In this chapter, you can see how four different companies all use the lead carpenter system in four slightly different— but effective — ways.

CASE STUDY ONE
Hartman Baldwin Design/Build
1

Location .... Claremont, California
Web Site .... www.hartmanbaldwin.com
Owners .... Devon Hartman (design)
                               Bill Baldwin (production)
Company Started 1981
Annual Sales Volume .... $2 million to $2.5 million
Number of Employees .... 15, which includes four lead carpenters, six field carpenters, three licensed architects, the two owners, and an office manager
Number of Jobs per Year 20
Average Size Job $100,000

It's easy to see why Hartman Baldwin has a reputation for being a bit brainy: Its town is home to seven private, highly acclaimed colleges. And because the firm's niche is high-end remodeling and restoration jobs, many of the firm's clients are academics, or wealthy, or both. Which means that the lead carpenters, who represent the company to the client for the bulk of a remodeling job, need some superb communication and people skills.

Says co-owner and production manager Bill Baldwin, "It's as important for a lead carpenter to know how to discuss the French Revolution with a client as it is to discuss the merits of Spanish, eclectic, and Arts & Crafts design." Hartman Baldwin lead carpenters are working inside the homes of a "heady" clientele, and so leads must behave in an intellectual manner. For instance, carpenters can have radios on the job, but radios must be tuned to National Public Radio or classical or jazz. There's no rock-and-roll allowed, and no Rush Limbaugh.

Attitude Is Everything

According to Baldwin, lead carpenters are not actually hired into the firm. Rather, people are brought into the company with rudimentary or perhaps no carpentry skills and are groomed from the first day to become a lead carpenter in the manner Hartman Baldwin wants. Nobody is called a helper or a laborer. If you're not a lead carpenter, you're a carpenter. Typically, it takes two or more years to reach the lead position. Once there, the wages are good, close to $25 an hour.

For Baldwin, the most important quality in a new hire is artistic vision and a strong sense of aesthetics. Lead carpenters are expected to take part in the design and details of the remodel. And as co-owner Devon Hartman points out, there's not a lot of finger-pointing in a design/build firm, but there is a lot of hand raising, as in "Hey, I've got an idea." Those aesthetically oriented ideas from leads are not only tolerated but expected.

Besides interest in aesthetics, lead carpenters at Hartman Baldwin need to have team ability, pride in workmanship, a lot of energy, intelligence, and education. Nearly all carpenters and leads have at least some college education.

Early Involvement

Because Hartman Baldwin is designing the project as well as building it, the lead carpenter (or "foreman," as he's called in this company) gets involved with the job at an early stage. Typically, the process starts with a feasibility study of a few different design options, along with preliminary estimates and a scope of work. If the client agrees with these, the feasibility portion is closed and the firm starts working drawings. At the point of engineering, it's sent out to the structural engineer.

When the engineering comes back, the lead carpenter who will be running the job is brought in. He's given a set of plans to take home, Baldwin takes a set of plans home, and the project manager (who designs the project) has a set of plans. All three red-mark the plans so they can resolve any questions they have about engineering. Then the lead, the project manager, and Baldwin sit down and discuss the architectural details that they'd like to see on the plans. Often the lead carpenter is brought in even before the job is officially sold.

When the plans are completed, the project manager schedules a pre-construction conference, often at the site, and it is then that the clients formally meet the lead carpenter.

Tweaking The System

As with most firms, Hartman Baldwin has struggled with the fact that because most lead carpenters want to get the job done as quickly as possible, they are prone to neglecting some of the paperwork. One problem has been with change orders, which are viewed by some carpenters as a sales function and therefore not part of their responsibilities. If they wanted to do sales, they figure, they'd be out running their own businesses.

Typically, change orders were verbally approved by the company owner and lead, but not written up in a timely manner, and too often not written up at all. This, of course, led to lost income for the company, and to a misconception by the client about how much the change extended the completion date. The company has tried several strategies to improve the situation. The latest approach is to motivate leads with a $25 reward for turning in a completed and signed change order form. The $25 "bribe" is added to the administrative costs of the change order, so the company doesn't lose money. So far, Baldwin says, the system is working.

Sharing The Profits

The company has a form of profit sharing, but it's at the discretion of the owners, rather than being based on any strict formula. The company looked at numerous ways to implement profit sharing on the basis of gross profit or net profit or tied to individual jobs. What they found was that the most effective approach was what Baldwin calls "the benevolent dictator school." Here's how it works: At the end of the year Hartman and Baldwin weigh out what jobs they have coming up, the state of their cash flow, and how the company did that year. From that, the sharing of profits is determined. Last year, they paid out $20,000, prorated according to hourly rate of pay and number of hours worked during the year.

An Ever-Evolving System

While Baldwin says he considers his firm to be on the cutting edge, he's amazed at what they learn every day. The company's management philosophy has been implemented for a long time, he says, and he believes the people in the lead carpenter positions are the right people. However, the lead carpenters are doing only about 80 percent of what the owners would like them to be doing in order to call the system perfect.

Part of the 20 percent lacking in lead carpenter performance is due to one of Baldwin's shortcomings, he says. "I just don't ask for help— I think I can do everything myself." But he recently realized that his "Papa Bear" position in the company was acting as a deterrent for others to make decisions on such challenges as change orders and dealing with difficult subs. A recent restructuring of his time and duties has allowed lead carpenters to assume greater responsibility. It's an ongoing process. Baldwin asks: "Am I done? How could I be done?"

CASE STUDY TWO
Remodeling Designs Inc.

2

Location ....Dayton, Ohio
Web site ....www.remodelingdesigns.com
Owners ....Michael Cordonnier, Joan Cordonnier,
                              Erich Eggers, Kelly Eggers
Year Company Started 1990
Specializes in ....Kitchens, baths, room additions
Annual Sales Volume ....$1 million
Number of Employees ....10, which includes one production manager and
                              five lead carpenters
Number of Jobs per Year 55
Average Size Job $22,000

When Mike Cordonnier and Erich Eggers started their remodeling company in 1990, they had some advantages and some disadvantages. On the up side, they both had some remodeling experience and college degrees in engineering. On the down side, they knew almost nothing about running a remodeling business, other than that they liked remodeling more than engineering. Luckily, they are both quick studies.

The company got started after Eggers and Cordonnier both remodeled their homes, and then a classmate from the University of Dayton asked them to remodel his home. After that, they decided, "Hey, we like this." For the first six years, the company operated out of Eggers' dining room and Cordonnier's basement and garage. Sales volume grew slowly and steadily and the pair rented their first office space in 1996.

In a similarly conservative manner, the company's structure and operations have evolved over the years. At first, both Eggers and Cordonnier were on job sites, sawing and pounding. Eventually, they learned about subcontractors, and by 1993 were able to allow Eggers to get into full-time sales, which he loved, and out of hands-on construction, which he didn't. "He got out of my hair," is how Cordonnier put it.

Sales and Production Separated

The shift left Cordonnier on the job site from 1993 to 1995, supervising the helper they had hired. "We're both conservative by nature,"

Cordonnier says to explain the steady, moderate pace of the company's growth. Then another guy was hired, who had more skills than a helper and could think for himself. He was therefore called a carpenter. In 1995, Eggers' brother-in-law, a skilled carpenter from Cleveland, was looking for a change, and brought his professional construction skills into the company. For Cordonnier, who realized he really liked designing and supervising more than pounding nails, hiring a highly skilled carpenter was a liberating experience: "That was my first inkling that there might be light at the end of the tunnel," he said.

Because Eggers was selling full-time, and was good at it, volume increased and another carpenter was hired, and another helper. By 1996, the company had several jobs going at once, with Cordonnier doing all the ordering, scheduling, and dealing with customers. At the same time, he had more and more design work lined up in the office, but not enough time to get it all done. Luckily, the carpenters were starting to take on more responsibility and were showing signs of becoming good job-site managers. Eggers and Cordonnier had heard of the lead carpenter system and Cordonnier decided to formally introduce it to his carpenters at the weekly company meeting, saying: "You guys are going to have to do more ordering and scheduling. I can't handle all the decisions. If a sub needs to be scheduled, you do it." The response couldn't have been more encouraging when the carpenters said, "We can handle all this. Why didn't you ask us before?"

Lead Carpenters in Full Swing

Today, the company has five lead carpenters, with Cordonnier acting as production manager. The hourly rate for leads ranges from $11 to $16 an hour. But the company considers its family-like atmosphere (both wives, also college graduates, have joined the company) and the generous employee benefits to be as important as wages. Health insurance is provided. There are seven paid holidays, and two weeks vacation after three years. Uniforms are provided. The company pays for lead carpenter training programs, and, in fact, prefers that the carpenter be working toward NARI's Certified Lead Carpenter designation. And when he is certified, he gets a $100 bonus. The week between Christmas and New Years is a company-wide paid holiday. And a year-end bonus is paid tied to performance and profit.

Because the company handles a lot of smaller jobs, the leads have a lot of time to work rather than just supervise a large project. For this reason, the owners prefer that lead carpenters have a lot of skills in the trades, including painting, drywall, carpentry, plumbing, electrical, and concrete.

The Process

Before a job begins, the lead meets with Cordonnier and coordinates the schedule, subcontractors, and materials. On larger jobs, Cordonnier will call in one of his more experienced leads to help with the estimate, asking: "How would you approach this job?" Cordonnier is not afraid to admit that a lead carpenter will know more than he does about construction. In fact, he counts on it.

Once the job starts, Cordonnier visits the site about once a week. If he visits more than that, he says, it undermines the confidence in the carpenter. The whole company keeps in touch with a two-way radio system. If a helper on one job needs to make a lumberyard run, he radios the other jobs to see if anyone else needs something. If an outside call needs to be made, the radio is used to call the office and office staff make it.

Recently, the company decided to change the title of the lead carpenter position to project manager. Even though the phrase "lead carpenter" perfectly explains the position's duties, other people, such as customers, do not understand that the lead carpenter is so much more than someone who pounds nails. To them, project manager is a more reassuring title.

Part of the company's success, Cordonnier believes, lies with a consistent, stable work force. He prides himself on having virtually no turnover. Besides good wages and benefits, he finds that employees want praise. They want to be acknowledged for good work. "I make a conscious effort to praise them," he says. And the relatively relaxed atmosphere of the company—no Saturdays, for instance—helps keep people around. As Cordonnier likes to say: "Without these guys, I'd be on skid row."

CASE STUDY THREE
HammerSmith, Inc.

3

Location	Decatur, Georgia
Web site	www.hammersmith.com
Owners	Warner McConaughey and Craig Kennedy
Year Company Started	1991
Specializes in	Design/build, high-end remodels
Annual Sales Volume	$2.9 million
Number of Employees	18, which includes one production manager, seven lead carpenters, one field carpenter, and three laborers
Number of Jobs per Year	45
Average Size Job	$50,000 to $80,000

Even though HammerSmith, Inc. is a relatively new company, created in 1991, its volume is already near $3 million, and it is poised to grow beyond that. The two owners have complementary skills and abilities: Warner McConaughey has 18 years of construction experience and was running a small remodeling company when he teamed up with Craig Kennedy, a certified public accountant who previously worked as the controller of a Seattle-based commercial construction business.

The company started using the lead carpenter system four years ago after reading about it in a trade publication. Until 1994, when the company grew to $800,000, the owners did all management/sales functions and had field employees that did all the construction work. There were usually three to four jobs going on at one time, and each employee had specialized skills, such as framing, drywall, or trim. Each morning, employees would be called and told where they were to be working that day. Those times are remembered in the company as times of chaos. Eventually, the owners realized that they needed to be freed up to sell other jobs instead of worrying about who was picking up the lumber, or when a sub was showing up. The lead carpenter system, where one carpenter would take full responsibility for each job and where that person could supervise the subs, seemed to be the answer.

Rocky Road to Lead Carpenter System

For HammerSmith, as for most companies doing nearly $1 million in volume, the transition into the lead carpenter system was not without difficulty. For instance, while several employees were good at their particular trade specialty, they did not have the skills or aptitude to become managers of jobs. Some had to be let go; others left voluntarily to work in jobs where their talents were better suited. Three carpenters from that time period stayed with the company and became lead carpenters.

For training, the managers have come to rely heavily on the NARI lead carpenter training program. Last year, half of the leads took the course, and this year the other half will attend. Of the seven current lead carpenters, three are former contractors. When a lead is newly hired into the company, he typically will be moved around for the first month to work with other leads in the company and learn how the system operates. The younger guys, with less construction experience, will also spend time helping the framers, the plumber, the electrician, and other trades.

Hiring Right

While carpentry and other building skills in a lead carpenter are important to the company, even more critical is how well a potential lead communicates and how he looks. The carpentry skills, if weak, can be taught, while ease and clarity of communication and professional appearance are much more difficult concepts to teach and grasp. Plus, the owners must have a feeling that the new hire is a person they can trust and the clients will trust.

At this time, HammerSmith jobs average $50,000, with a few as high as $100,000. And getting into higher-end remodels and restoration jobs— "up to a million bucks," says production manager Wright Marshall—is the company's goal. Already the company and its leads have a reputation in the Atlanta area for working well with difficult, demanding clients who need a lot of hand-holding.

And this is where the lead carpenter system, as HammerSmith uses it, really makes a difference. The unique factor is that a lead carpenter stays on the job all the time. Even if two jobs are only a half mile from each other, a lead will not supervise two projects. Of course, this policy costs the company money, but the owners believe that this policy will bring them the higher-end jobs they covet. "Baby-sitting the client" is not a negative concept in this company's culture. And in the golden future, many jobs will be so large that the company expects that the lead carpenter will not wear a tool belt, but will spend all his time planning, supervising, ordering, and interacting with the client.

How It Works

After the contract is signed, the production manager schedules and coordinates the first two weeks of the project in terms of ordering the initial materials, setting up the framing package, and planning the demolition and any other early work. At that time, the product selections are made with the help of an interior designer, including the fixtures and appliances.

During this pre-job phase, the lead starts a job file and reviews all contract specs and drawings, the estimate, and the job schedule, and relays any expected problems to the architect and production manager.

A week before the job is to start, the production manager, salesman, architect and lead carpenter gather with the client to have a "pass-the-baton" meeting. This is where the lead is established as the contact person for the client. The lead is walked through the project to make sure he has a full understanding of its intent and intricacies. He writes any special considerations and priorities in a job book. With all this preparation the lead carpenter is able to "hit the ground running" when he starts the actual job. He takes over all the ordering and scheduling for the rest of the job and is responsible for the successful completion of the job, which means coming in on time and on budget, and meeting a standard of high quality.

For change orders over $100, the production manager steps in and sets a price for the customer. This eliminates the lead's tendency to undercharge for changes.

The best element of the lead carpenter system for HammerSmith is the continuity it offers between the client and the company, especially on renovation jobs, where client contact is so intensive. The system also brings much welcome connection between the job site and the office. The down side of the system occurs on larger jobs when there is so much supervision necessary that the lead isn't able to accomplish much carpentry work. Of course, when a job gets very large, that is to be expected. But there are mid-sized jobs where spending three-quarters of the day working with the plumber can be frustrating for a lead who was expecting to be driving nails that day.

Pay and Benefits on the Rise

The top leads in the company currently earn $16 an hour, plus benefits, including a tool program in which the company pays half for every tool that costs more than $100. And they expect to start up a profit sharing system. So far, leads tend to stay with the company for a little over two years. The managers would like to improve upon that, and have been raising benefits as profits have gotten better. Also, as the company grows and matures, employment with it will be perceived as more of a career path, rather than just a stopping place on the way to a bigger company.

System Still Changing

According to the company owners, their lead carpenter system is in its adolescent stage, still growing and changing. For instance, the production manager was only brought into the company last year. And with seven lead carpenters, that position was desperately needed. According to production manager Wright Marshall, if the owners knew then what they know now, they would have hired the production manager first, and then developed the lead carpenter system.

A continuing challenge for Marshall, who has a background in building tract homes, is encouraging the lead carpenters to sub out such tasks as framing and trim work, instead of doing it themselves. What Marshall and the owners want is for the jobs to be finished more quickly. Indeed, the owners look forward to a day where the leads do not swing a hammer at all. Perhaps in readiness for that day, the managers already call their lead carpenters by another name: project managers.

CASE STUDY FOUR
Sass Construction Inc.

4

Location .... Excelsior, Minnesota
Web Sit .... www.sassconstruction.com
Owners .... Mark A. Sass, president
                        Christine Sass, vice president
Year Company Started 1980
Annual Sales Volume .... $1.2 million
Specializing in .... 60% residential remodeling, 40% insurance work
Number of Employees .... 12, which includes three lead carpenters (looking
                        for a fourth), one field carpenter, one helper
Number of Jobs per Year ...... About 150
Average Size Job .... $20,000 (for remodels, insurance work usually
                        less)

Sass Construction was started by Mark and Christine Sass in 1980. It makes sense that the company does 40% insurance work; Mark worked in the insurance industry for seven years before hanging out his "Sass Construction" shingle. Christine was a bookkeeper for a car rental agency. For the first ten years, Sass Construction was operated from the couple's home. In 1990, the company moved to an office, and Christine started to work part time in the office, mainly doing payroll every two weeks, and full time raising their three children.

Shortly after that, in the mid 1990s, it occurred to Mark Sass and production manager John McGowan that the lead carpenter system might work well in their company. They obtained information from the NARI lead carpenter program after they heard about it at a trade seminar. When they reached a sales volume of about $800,000 a year, they realized that to grow further they would need to transfer on-site responsibility for supervising subs, planning, scheduling inspections, and dealing with the clients.

Doubts About Paperwork

At first, the company's carpenters were concerned that there would be too much paperwork. At the same time, the company's managers realized that a tight system for paperwork would be critical to make it all work. Paperwork for leads includes a weekly breakdown of what labor is done in what category (concrete, plumbing, painting, etc.) on each job. One triplicate form, titled "On-Site Job Communication," allows messages and replies to be transmitted smoothly. Here's how it works:

1) the "addressor" writes a message on the left side of the top sheet, which is white, and leaves it on the pad;

2) the "addressee" writes a reply on the right side of the top sheet, and takes the second sheet, which is yellow, for his records; and

3) the addressor notes the reply, leaves the white sheet for a permanent record, and takes the third sheet, which is pink, for his records.

Getting a Job Started

The lead carpenter is brought into the project as soon as the contract is signed and a down payment is made. In a "baton-passing" job-site meeting with the clients, production manager, salesman, and lead carpenter, the contract and scope of work are reviewed line by line to make sure there are no questions or confusion. The smallest detail is addressed. Afterward, either that day or the next day, the lead carpenter comes into the office and spends at least four hours with management to plan and plot out the job. They decide what materials will be needed, which subs, and other details.

Because many jobs are smaller, such as insurance work after storms, each of the company's three leads may be in charge of three or four jobs at a time. Obviously, they cannot be on each job at all times, and usually that's not necessary as subs come in to do their work. This frees up the leads to all work together when needed on a larger, more complex job, thereby bringing all of the company's construction experience to bear instead of having one lead and a number of helpers.

Change orders are discussed between the lead carpenters and the clients, but when it comes to pricing, the production manager takes over. Everybody prefers this to having the lead give the client a price on change orders.

Pay and Benefits

At Sass Construction, lead carpenters are paid $16 an hour, plus truck reimbursement, health insurance, and paid holidays and vacations. Bonuses are paid at the end of the year based on company performance, although not tied to a specific percentage. In a good year, the bonuses go up.

The benefits of the lead carpenter system are many. It brings continuity to a job, which pleases clients. The lead has his finger on the pulse of a job at all times. The production manager doesn't have to "baby-sit" each job. And because someone is on top of all the details, finishing up a job is much easier.

The downside is that it takes longer to finish a job. At least it seems like it does, especially when you add on at least one entire day for planning at the front end. But because in the past the company often saw six-week jobs drag out to seven or eight weeks because of bad planning, that one day now seems like a small price to pay.

Another challenge is that every lead does things just a little differently, such as filling out the paperwork. This sometimes creates a little confusion. However, instead of trying to force everyone into the same mold, the company adjusts to each lead's style, up to a point. And there's not a lot of turnover; only one lead has left the company to go into another trade.

Finding New Leads a Challenge

The final down side is the lack of trained people to hire. The company would love to hire another lead carpenter, but after months of looking and checking and interviewing, it has still not made that hire. The lack of leads hampers them after a big storm when there's a lot of insurance work to be done and the company is struggling to keep its regular remodeling jobs going as well.

The company has no formal training program for leads, but relies heavily on the job description, careful hiring, and employee attendance at seminars on building codes, lead carpenter systems, and energy issues.

When John McGowan is asked what is unique about Sass Construction's lead carpenter system, he says, "Well, I guess what's unique about it is that it works!" Apparently it does; the company's volume has increased 50% since the system was set in place. McGowan says, "We try to be thorough from day one all the way through. We have a mature system. I think we have a pretty good thing going here." ◪

Appendix A

Forms for Job-site Management

Job Start Checklist
(Received from Sales Department)

Customer:_____   Contract Date:_____

Salesperson:_____   Start Date:_____

- ☐ Plans
- ☐ Contract
- ☐ Zoning OK
- ☐ Permit
- ☐ "Before" photographs: Review if complete
- ☐ Review draw schedule
- ☐ Final computer spec. required
- ☐ Subcontractor and material bid
  - ☐ Excavation
  - ☐ Electrical
  - ☐ Plumbing
  - ☐ HVAC
  - ☐ Masonry
  - ☐ Windows/Doors
  - ☐ Marble/Tile
  - ☐ Hardware
  - ☐ Floor covering
  - ☐ Cabinets
  - ☐ Wall finishes
  - ☐ Painting
  - ☐ Roofing
  - ☐ Insulation
- ☐ Items that need to be selected/approved allowances
  - ☐ Light fixtures
  - ☐ Plumbing fixtures
  - ☐ Tile/Marble/Corian
  - ☐ Paint color
  - ☐ Floor covering
  - ☐ Shower doors
  - ☐ Appliances
  - ☐ Hardware
  - ☐ Cabinets/layout
  - ☐ Brick
  - ☐ Door
  - ☐ Trim detail

_____

_____

_____

_____

_____

_____

_____

_____

_____

_____

ALLOWANCE/SELECTION LIST

	Selection	Allowance	OK
1. Bricks	_____	_____	_____
2. Roof material	_____	_____	_____
3. Siding	_____	_____	_____
4. Door hardware	_____	_____	_____
5. Plumbing fixtures	_____	_____	_____
6. Electrical fixtures	_____	_____	_____
7. Wallpaper	_____	_____	_____
8. Paneling	_____	_____	_____
9. Painting	_____	_____	_____
10. Carpet	_____	_____	_____
11. Vinyl	_____	_____	_____
12. Ceramic tile	_____	_____	_____
13. Wood flooring	_____	_____	_____
14. _____		_____	_____
15. _____		_____	_____
16. _____		_____	_____
17. _____		_____	_____
18. _____		_____	_____
19. _____		_____	_____
20. _____		_____	_____
21. _____		_____	_____
22. _____		_____	_____
23. _____		_____	_____

SPECIAL ORDER CHECKLIST

Item	Lead Time	Date Ordered	Date Expected	Supplier	Salesperson	Quoted Cost
Appliances						
Cabinets						
Doors						
Electrical fixtures						
Fabricate steel						
Floor covering						
Hardware (specify)						
Marble						
Medicine cabinets						
Millwork trim						
Plumbing fixtures						
Tile						
Tops						
Windows						

PROJECT SCHEDULE

Project: _____

Calendar Period: _____

Page _____ of _____

Description of Work

#

☐ = Projected

PRECONSTRUCTION TOOL CHECKLIST

Job Name:_____   Lead Carpenter:_____

Quantity	Description	Quantity	Description
	Air hoses		Shovel, flat
	Air compressor		Shovel, round
	Broom, straw		Sledge hammer
	Broom, push		Snow fence
	Caulk		Staple gun
	Change Order pad		Tape, duct
	Construction adhesive		Tape, masking
	Demo hammer		Time cards
	Framing gun		Transit
	Hammer drill		Trash can
	Jack hammer		Weekly reports
	Knack box		Wheelbarrow
	Ladder, step		Nails (list type)
	Ladder, extension		
	Lights		
	Masonite		Saw blades (list type)
	Phone box		
	Phone		
	Pick		Special hardware (list type)
	Plastic		
	Ramset		
	Rosin paper		Other:
	Scaffolding		
	Shims		
	Shop vac		

JOB SITE ASSESSMENT FORM

Job Name:_____ Contract #:_____ Date:_____

Section 1. Site Prep

Locate:
- ☐ Trash pile
- ☐ Lockbox
- ☐ Bathroom
- ☐ Material storage, interior
- ☐ Material storage, exterior

- ☐ Landscape protection
- ☐ Parking
- ☐ Job phone
- ☐ Dust protection assessed
- ☐ Floor protection assessed
- ☐ Furniture/breakables to be removed

Section 2: Site Conditions

☐ Wall finish condition: _____

_____

_____

☐ Floor condition: _____

_____

_____

☐ Ceiling condition: _____

_____

_____

☐ Windows & doors condition: _____

_____

_____

☐ Trim condition: _____

_____

_____

☐ Bath fixtures: _____

    Water supply: _____

    Drain: _____

    Finishes: _____

☐ Kitchen – Cabinets: _____

    Water supply: _____

    Drain: _____

    Countertops: _____

    Appliances: _____

☐ Driveway condition: _____

_____

☐ Landscaping: _____

Section 3. Site Survey *(continued)*

1. Basement/Foundation: _____   Type: _____

    Condition:

               Finish: _____   Moist: _____

               Height: _____   Plumb: _____

2. Attic: _____   Type: _____

    Condition:

               Rafters: _____   Joists: _____

                                    Utilities: _____

3. Roof: _____   Type: _____

    Condition:

               Gutters: _____   Water protection?_____

               Soffit: _____   Fascia:_____

4. Floors: Alignment (level?)_____   Finish condition: _____

5. Trim: Baseboard type: _____   Size: _____

        Casing type: _____   Size: _____

6. Doors & Windows: Door: _____   Head height: _____

                  Window:_____   Head height: _____

                                     Sill height: _____

Lead Carpenter:_____   Date: _____

I have read this Job Site Assessment and agree with its contents.

Owner: _____   Date: _____

Owner: _____   Date: _____

WEEKLY TIME CARD

Name:_____   Week Ending:_____

Day	Job	Description	Code	Start	Stop	Hours
Wed						
Lunch						
Thurs						
Lunch						
Fri						
Lunch						
Mon						
Lunch						
Tues						
Lunch						

EVERYDAY CONSTRUCTION
Job Log

Project: _____

Weather: ☐ Fair ☐ Overcast ☐ Rain ☐ Snow

Job Number: _____

Temperature: ☐ 0-30 ☐ 30-50 ☐ 50-60 ☐ 60&up

Lead Carpenter: _____

Wind: ☐ Still ☐ Moderate ☐ High

___Excavators	___Plumbers	___Security/Audio	___Carpet Installers
___Footings	___Electricians	___Stone Masons	___Vinyl Installers
___Block Work	___Heat & A/C	___Gutters & Downspouts	___Cntrtop Installers
___Exterminators	___Insulators	___Hardwood Installers	___Mirror/Shwr/Hdwr.
___Laborers	___Roofers	___Ceram. Tile Installer	___Driveway Installers
___Conc. Flatwork	___Drywallers	___Trim Carpenters	___Cleaners
___Frame Carpent.	___Brick Layers	___Painters	___Landscapers
___St. Fabricators	___Siding Installer	___Special Millwork	___Others_____

Visitors: (i.e., Homeowner, Architect, Office Personnel, Construction Manager)

Time	Name	Remarks
_____	_____	_____
_____	_____	_____
_____	_____	_____

Hopkins & Porter Labor:

Name	Time	Total Hrs	Rate	Cost	Item Code/ Work Completed
_____	___ to ___	_____	_____	_____	_____
_____	___ to ___	_____	_____	_____	_____
_____	___ to ___	_____	_____	_____	_____
_____	___ to ___	_____	_____	_____	_____
_____	___ to ___	_____	_____	_____	_____

Total Cost:_____ Cumulative:_____ Budget:_____

Homeowner Remarks: _____

Extra Work/Changes Requested by Homeowner: _____

Selections/Decisions to be made by Homeowner: _____
_____ by (Date):_____

Daily Notes: _____
_____
_____
_____
_____
_____

Reviewed by supervisor:_____ Date:_____

STIPULATED SUM
Change Order #_____

Job Name & Number: _____   Date: _____

Prepared By: _____

Change Description *Note: Please use Sub name*	Phase #	Labor hours x $	Material Cost	Sub Cost/ Name	Total Cost	M.U. @ 20%	Sale Price

Labor Charge: Lead Carpenter @. . . . . $ # of Days:_____   Total:_____

Helper @ . . . . $

Date entered into Computer: _____

_____

FIELD CHANGE ORDER

We agree to make change(s) or perform additional work at the request and orders of:

Name		Date:	
Address		Job #:	
City, State, Zip Code		Date of Existing Contract:	
Job Address		Job Phone:	

hereinafter referred to as Owner, for work performed at premises set forth above. It is proposed to make changes(s) or perform additional work as follows:

_____

_____

_____

_____

_____

_____

_____

_____

_____

_____

_____

_____

_____

_____

_____

_____

_____

Additional work specified above becomes part of and is to be performed under the same conditions as the existing contract between Contractor and Owner when signed Change Order is received by Contractor.

_____	_____	_____	_____
Company Representative	Date	Owner	Date

PRECONSTRUCTION MEETING CHECKLIST

Job Name:_____ Date:_____

People Present: _____

Things to take to meeting:

Stamped plans
Business cards
Specs and Contract

1. Purpose of meeting: Introduce entire "team."

2. What do clients expect from the project? From us?

3. Any special considerations for clients? Other people to be aware of?

4. Inform clients of dust, dirt, noise, inconvenience. Discuss.

5. Everyday issues:

    a. Job hours:

    b. Bathroom

    c. Keys/security

    d. Telephone

    e. Trash

    f. Job sign

    g. Location of utilities (please clear access)

    h. Change Order policy (takes time, slows job, signed forms)

    i. List of salvage items

    j. Emergency pager number

    k. Smoking policy

    l.

    m.

    n.

    o.

    p.

Phone Numbers

His Work:

Her Work:

Home:

6. Selections that still need to be made:

    a. _____

    b. _____

    c. _____

    d. _____

    e. _____

    f. _____

7. Start date and what happens between now and then:

8. Discuss importance of GOOD COMMUNICATION!

9. Tour of home.

ID	Task Name			
17	First Floor deck			
18	First Floor walls			
19	Second Deck			
20	Second Floor walls			
21	Roof and Ceiling			
22	CABINET AND APPLIANCE SELECTION DUE (DDD)			
23	Exterior Trim			
24	Install Fascia			
25	Install Windows/Doors			
26	Stucco Siding			
27	Build Powder Room Wall:Remove kitchen cabinets as needed to create a dust barrier			
28	Dust Barriers/Interior Demo: Install plastic dust barrier with zippers as needed for access			
29	Demo Openings to House			
30	Roofing			
31	Porches			
32	Deck			

PROJECT SCHEDULE: LIST FORMAT

ID	Task Name	Duration	Start	Finish	Predecessors	Resource Names
1						
2						
3						
4						
5						
6						
7						
8						
9						
10						
11						
12						
13						
14						
15						
16						
17						
18						
19						
20						
21						
22						
23						
24						
25						
26						
27						

Appendix B

Lead Carpenter Survey

INTRODUCTION

*O*VER THE COURSE OF SEVERAL SEMINARS *I* HAVE GIVEN RECENTLY, *I* SURVEYED A cross section of attendees—lead carpenters and contractors—to determine how different companies in the United States are using the lead carpenter system.

These contractors and lead carpenters come from the West Coast, the Midwest, and the Northeast. The questions were presented on paper and tallied later. The questions focused on current company policies such as wages, benefits, and responsibilities. In total, 65 lead carpenters and 37 contractors responded to the survey. —*Timothy Faller*

SURVEY QUESTION #1:

What percentage of the lead carpenter's time is still spent in actual production on the site?

Percentage of time spent in production	Percentage of Respondents
Less than 20%	0%
20 to 30%	1%
30 to 40%	2%
40 to 50%	2%
50 to 60%	4%
60 to 70%	13%
70 to 80%	19%
80 to 90%	27%
90 to 99%	29%
100%	3%

SURVEY QUESTION #2:

Which duties are you (the lead carpenter) responsible for on the site?

Duties on Site	Percentage of Respondents
Framing	100%
Client Meetings	73%
Ordering Materials	90%
Scheduling Subs	59%
Finish Trim	100%
Writing Change Orders	47%
Scheduling the Job	50%
Contracting with Subs	15%
Supervising Subs	78%

SURVEY QUESTION #3:

How long have you been a lead carpenter?

Number of Years	Percentage of Respondents
Less than 2	40.5%
Two to four	22%
Four to six	15.5%
Six to eight	8%
Eight to ten	8%
More than ten	6%

Survey Question #4:

What was your starting wage?

Starting Wage (per hour)	Percentage of Respondent
Less than $5	1.5%
$5 to $8	17%
$8 to $10	15.5%
$10 to $12	12%
$12 to $14	15.5%
$14 to $16	14%
$16 to $18	18%
More than $18	7%

Survey Question #5:

What are your current wages?

Starting Wage (per hour)	Percentage of Respondents
Less than $5	0%
$5 to $8	0%
$8 to $10	3%
$10 to $12	10%
$12 to $14	14.5%
$14 to $16	30.5%
$16 to $18	18%
More than $18	24%

Survey Question #6:

What is the highest rate you (the contractor) will pay for a lead carpenter?

Highest Wage (per hour)	Percentage of Respondents
Less than $16	15%
$16 to $18	19.5%
$18 to $20	23%
$20 to $25	38.5%
More than $25	4%

Survey Question #7:

Which of these benefits do you receive as part of your compensation?

Benefit Received	Percentage of Respondents
Health Insurance	65.6%
Dental Insurance	27.5%
Life Insurance	26.5%
Tool Purchase Allowance	29.5%
Paid Holidays	67.5%
Less than 5 vacation days	36%
Five or more vacation days	40%
Bonuses	60%

Survey Question #8:

Does your company provide training?

Provides training	Percentage of Respondents
Yes	75%
No	25%

Appendix C

Lead Carpenter Training Segments

As discussed in Chapter 5, effective training of lead carpenters is vital to the success of the system and the growth and profits of your company. At Hopkins and Porter we have developed a training program that consists of 16 segments on different topics relevant to our lead carpenters. Each segment can stand alone, or all sixteen can be conducted sequentially over the course of, say, 16 months. Each of the segments can be completed in about 45 minutes.

We are still developing and fine-tuning this program. You can use it as a starting point for developing your own training program, but undoubtedly, your company's specific needs and program will differ from ours. Also, because training is an ongoing process, several of the segments presented here contain follow-up exercises. I encourage you to come up with additional follow-up or practice exercises to help make training an active part of your company.

TRAINING SEGMENT #1

Topic: Mission Statement and Policies

Trainer:

Preparation: Careful preparation of how to explain the purpose and use of a mission statement to a group of people who are not trained to think that way. Develop some examples that they can identify with that reflect your mission statement.

Materials Needed by Trainer: Copies of all policies
a. Mission Statement
b. Job Completion
c. Miss Utility Markings
d. Tipping for Company Employees
e. Side Work for Company Employees
f. Change Orders
g. Job Inspection
h. Substance Abuse

Content: • Detailed discussion of Mission Statement and how it affects the field.
• Discuss how policies were written.
• Discuss why there are policies and how they affect the field.
• Discuss where the policies are kept and how to access them as needed.

Follow-up Exercise:

Timetable: 45 minutes

Actual Time:

Date of Training:

Trainer's Notes:

TRAINING SEGMENT #2

Topic: Company Habits

Trainer:

Preparation: Think through the habits that you want everyone in the company to adopt. Some examples are reflected below.

Materials Needed by Trainer: Agenda for training meeting

Content:
- Clean job site.   *Daily:*   broom clean, locked up, neat and tidy, trash pile neat,

                       Friday: broom clean, all material stored, tools up and safe, ladders stored, locked up, trash pile removed
- Appropriate dress: Company T-shirt or sweat shirt, pants that are not torn, appropriate shoes.
- Being on time: Arrive on job 6:45 a.m., set up tools, begin work at 7:00 a.m., clean up and leave job
- Breaks   15-min. morning break

                         30-min. lunch break
- Participation in company meetings.
- Hand in paperwork on time: time cards, receipts, work orders, etc.

Timetable: 45 minutes

Actual Time:

Date of Training:

Trainer's Notes:

TRAINING SEGMENT #3

Topic: Attitudes

Trainer:

Preparation: Spend time thinking about the appearance that you want the company to have and the way that attitudes reflect that. Be sure you understand the relationship and can communicate it to others. Practice on someone else.

Materials Needed by Trainer: Agenda for the meeting

Content:
- Discuss the need for good attitudes and what bad attitudes do to the company.
- Discuss how to maintain a positive attitude in spite of negative experiences.
- Discuss service as an attitude. How does the attitude of service display itself?
- Discuss developing teamwork as an attitude. How does this attitude show itself?

(Every company should look carefully at the attitude or attitudes they want displayed and train for those attitudes. This training should not be devoted to discussing one person's attitude.)

Timetable: 45 minutes

Actual Time:

Date of Training:

Trainer's Notes:

TRAINING SEGMENT #4

Topic: Job Costing

Trainer:

Preparation:

Materials Needed by Trainer: Samples of the reports we want the field to recognize

Content:
- Explain how to understand an estimate.
- Explain why the estimate may say one thing and the specs another.
- Explain how to use an estimate in the field.
- Explain the dollar amounts associated with each position.
- Discuss how the information received in the office gets into the reports.
- Explain why careful coding is important.
- Explain how to read reports.
- Review all terms found on the reports.
- Show how we arrive at Gross Profit and Net Profit.
- Show how missing the budget affects Net Profit.

Follow-up Exercise: Give the leads a problem to solve involving gross profit and net profit and final real profit.

Timetable: This training may take two sessions

Actual Time:

Date of Training:

Trainer's Notes:

TRAINING SEGMENT #5

Topic: Proper Job Planning

Trainer:

Preparation:

Materials Needed by Trainer: Forms for planning a job

Content: • Review the contents of the job folder.
  • Review how each piece is important.
  • Discuss the benefits of doing a material list early.
  • Discuss the Lead Carpenter's role in the preconstruction conference.
  • Discuss the benefit of doing a schedule as it relates to good planning.
  • Review what the company allows as it relates to time and place of review.

Timetable: 45 minutes

Actual Time:

Date of Training:

Trainer's Notes:

TRAINING SEGMENT #6

Topic: Scheduling

Trainer:

Preparation:

Materials Needed by Trainer: Training Manual on scheduling

Content:
- Discuss the importance of scheduling by the numbers — not on the fly.
- Discuss the impact on bottom line of missing the schedule.
- Discuss how to schedule a job.
- Discuss the problems avoided by proper scheduling.
- Discuss how to follow a schedule.

Follow-up Exercise: Have the leads do a schedule for a sample job.

Timetable: 45 minutes

Actual Time:

Date of Training:

Trainers Notes:

TRAINING SEGMENT #7

Topic: Job-Site Safety

Trainer:

Preparation:

Materials Needed by Trainer: Safety Policy, Manual

Content:
- Who is responsible for the safety of a job site?
- What do you do in the case of an accident?
- What do you do when someone else on the job is practicing unsafe practices?
- What safety practices are most critical on our sites?
- What is the penalty for not practicing safety?

Follow-up Exercise:

Timetable: 45 minutes

Actual Time:

Date of Training:

Trainer's Notes:

TRAINING SEGMENT #8

Topic: Change Orders

Trainer:

Preparation: Prepare some sample change order situations that have occurred recently so that everyone can identify with them.

Materials Needed by Trainer: Change Order forms, Change Order calculating forms, sample Change Order Report (any forms that you want the leads to use for change orders.)

Content:
- Discuss the benefits and dangers of change orders.
- Discuss the role we want the Lead Carpenters to play in change orders.
- Explain how to use the Change Order Field Form.
- Explain the Change Order report Form.
- Explain how to use the Change Order calculating forms.
- Discuss when to turn it over to the salesman.

Follow-up Exercise: Give an example of a change order and ask participants to calculate a CO and present to an "owner." Have another Lead be the owner.

Change Order Exercise: You are building a single story kitchen addition with three windows, each is 2'0" x 3'0." There is no siding on the addition yet and the wiring has been started but not completed. The windows are installed. They are wood with brick mold exterior. The clients want to move one window to the left 3 feet. There is clear wall space available. How much should you charge and how would you "present" this to the client?

Timetable: 45 minutes

Actual Time:

Date of Training:

Trainer's Notes:

TRAINING SEGMENT #9

Topic: Final Completion of a Job

Trainer:

Preparation:

Materials Needed by Trainer: Final Completion List form, Final Completion policy

Content:
- Discuss the company policy on Final Completion.
- Review the role we want the Lead Carpenter to play in the policy.
- Review the other players in the policy.
- Discuss the importance of signatures on the list.

Follow-up Exercise: Role-play different parts of the plan.

Timetable: 45 minutes

Actual Time:

Date of Training:

Trainer's Notes:

TRAINING SEGMENT #10

Topic: Working with Inspectors

Trainer:

Preparation:

Materials Needed by Trainer: Role play scenarios

Content:
- Be ready for an inspection.
- Be courteous.
- Clean site.
- Learn names.
- Ask about future code changes.
- Discuss the role the inspectors play and try to change the attitude of the carpenters to work with, rather than against, the inspectors.

Follow-up Exercise: Have the carpenters share the things they have learned about working with inspectors.

Timetable: 45 minutes

Actual Time:

Date of training:

Trainer's Notes:

TRAINING SEGMENT #11

Topic: People Skills

Trainer:

Preparation:

Materials Needed by Trainer: Role play scenarios, training notebook.

Content:
- Working with homeowners.
- Setting expectations.
- Meeting expectations that have been set by others.
- The importance of a clean work site.
- Fixing mistakes and problems as they happen.
- How do you deal with an "in your face" client?
- Running a site meeting.
- Setting up a communication center.

Follow-up Exercise: Use the role playing here. This may take two sessions to really impact the employees.

Timetable: 45 minutes

Actual Time:

Date of Training:

Trainer's Notes:

TRAINING SEGMENT #12

Topic: Managing Employees

Trainer:

Preparation: Take time to develop the role-playing situations that you will use. Draw off real situation to enhance the value.

Materials Needed by Trainer: Role play scenarios

Content:
- The importance of the one-man crew.
- What are the Lead Carpenter's responsibilities on the site as far as managing the employees?
- Hire and fire responsibilities: are there any?
- How can the Lead maximize efficiency of site?
    - Lists
    - Meetings
    - Disciplined Breaks
    - Divide job into mini jobs
- Goal setting on a job site.

Follow-up Exercise: Give the leads a little "pop quiz" that gets them to write down or regurgitate some of the info.

Timetable: 45 minutes

Actual Time:

Date of Training:

Trainer's Notes:

TRAINING SEGMENT #13

Topic: Working with Subcontractors

Trainer:

Preparation:

Materials Needed by Trainer: Role play scenarios, sub memos

Content:
- Process of getting a Subcontractor when you want him.
- Subcontractor review.
- Who's really in charge?
- Getting the most from a sub.
    - Planning ahead
    - Being ready
    - Clean site
    - Team atmosphere

Timetable: 45 minutes

Actual Time:

Date of Training:

Trainer's Notes:

TRAINING SEGMENT #14

Topic: Material Management

Trainer:

Preparation:

Materials Needed by Trainer: Sample material lists

Content: • Discuss the benefits of and need to make lists early in the job.
   • Discuss delivery vs. pick up, emphasis $$$.
   • Discuss the need for keeping a record of all deliveries.
   • Discuss the need to record accurately items ordered, both the items and where they came from.
   • Discuss the need to check every delivery for accuracy.
   • Discuss protecting materials from the weather.

Follow-up Exercise: Make a material list for a sample job and estimate the value of the package. See who comes closest to an actual take off and pricing.

Timetable: 45 minutes

Actual Time:

Date of Training:

Trainer's Notes:

TRAINING SEGMENT #15

Topic: Job Logs

Trainer:

Preparation:

Materials Needed by Trainer: Sample job log, guidelines for job logs

Content: • Discuss why job logs are critical.
  Legal record
  Record of daily progress
  Evaluation of subs, service, etc.
• Show how to fill them in.
• What will the office do with them?

Follow-up Exercise: Have the leads fill in a job log and check them. Give them the scenario for the day that they are filling out.

Timetable: 45 minutes

Actual Time:

Date of Training:

Trainer's Notes:

TRAINING SEGMENT #16

Topic: Time Cards

Trainer:

Preparation:

Materials Needed by Trainer: Sample time cards, written layout of time card description

Content:
- Discuss the need for accurate, detailed time cards.
- Show sample of incorrect time card.
- Show sample of corrected time card.
- Show how the time cards are handled in the office.
- What is the law regarding overtime and filling in time cards fully?

Timetable: 45 minutes

Actual Time:

Date of Training:

Trainer's Notes:

Index

A
Advertising, for lead carpenter, 62-63
Allowances, form, 95
Architects, working with, 135
Authority, lead carpenter as, 36, 148, 149-150

B
Blueprints. *See* **Plans.**
Bonuses, 67-68, 147, 184. *See also* **Employee benefits.**
Budget,
> job-costing training segment, 189
> sharing information with lead, 19, 38, 81-89, 145

C
Carpentry,
> lead performing, 16
> time spent by lead, 182

Case studies, 153-163
Change orders,
> forms in field, 105, 107-108
> giving away work, 32-33, 150
> motivating leads to do paperwork, 155
> training segment, 193

Changing leads mid-job, 36-37
Clients
> communication with, 30-31, 35, 133
> concerns of, 5, 92, 94
> difficult, 34, 132, 159-160
> hot buttons for, 94
> management of, 132-133
> responsibilities, 105, 109
> want to deal with owner, 36-37
> *See also* **Customer service; Preconstruction conference.**

Communication
> between lead carpenter and clients, 30-31, 35, 133
> forms for, 24
> meetings, 23
> people skills, training segment, 196
> skills of lead carpenter, 22, 35, 159
> verbal, 24
> *See also* **Clients; Team, company as.**

Company habits, training segment, 187

Compensation

    of lead carpenters, 33, 66-68

    salary survey, 183

    salary vs. wages, 67

    See also **Employee benefits.**

Completion dates, and one-man crew, 36, 38, 126

Cost control

    overhead, 84, 85

    production, 84, 86-89

Crew size. *See* **Labor, one-man crew.**

Custom building, 4-5

Customer service, 31, 35. *See also* **Clients.**

D

Delegation

    and client issues, 36-37

    and loss of control, 33

    of control, 19

Down time, for lead carpenters, 147

E

Employee attitudes, training segment, 188

Employee benefits

    bonuses, 67-68, 147, 163, 184

    health insurance, 67, 157, 163, 184

    profit sharing, 68, 155

    retirement plan, 67

    survey of, 184

    tool purchase reimbursement, 160, 184

    training programs, 157

    vacation and sick days, 157, 163, 184

    vehicle reimbursement, 163

Employee policies, training segment, 186

Employees

    evaluating, 48

    managing, training segment, 197

    motivation of, 122-123

    skills needed to manage, 21

    supervision of, 121-123

Estimate

    evaluation of, 139-140

    in job folder, 101

Extras. *See* **Change orders.**

F

Final completion, training segment, 194

Firing employees, 20, 146

Fiscal management chart, 82

G

Gross profit. *See* **Profit.**

Growth

      and loss of good service, 29

      and need for lead carpenter system, 3, 7-9, 12, 18-19

      with production manager, 11

H

Handyman service, using down time for, 144

Hiring

      interviewing, 44-45

      lead carpenters, 37, 61-66, 144, 145-146, 148-149, 159, 163

      promoting current employees, 44-45

      questions, sample, 65

      See also **Interviewing.**

I

Indirect costs. *See* **Overhead.**

Inspectors

      working with, 133-135

      working with, training segment, 195

Interpersonal skills, 21

Interviewing

      continuous process, 66

      current employees, 44-45

      legal considerations, 66

      skills, 64-65

      See also **Hiring.**

J

Job-costing. *See* **Budget.**

Job costing training segment, 189

Job descriptions

      for contractor, 43

      for lead carpenters, 43-44, 47, 51-60, 62

      for whole company, 20

      See also **Lead carpenter, responsibilities.**

Job folder, 98-109

Job log, 105-106

Job log training segment, 200

Job planning,

      checklist for, 93

      job folder, 98, 101, 105

      material takeoffs, 109-110

      plan evaluation, 97-98

      preconstruction meeting, 110-112, 115

      preliminary, 91-94

      responsibility for, 16

      scheduling, 115-117

      site assessment, 94, 97

      training segment, 190

Job-site

    assessment, 94-97

    assessment form, 102-103, 105.

    office setup, 17

    See also **Site assessment.**

Job start checklist, 93

L

Labor, efficient use of, 27-28, 86, 121-122, 145

Labor burden worksheet, 87

Labor costs, control of, 84, 86-87

Lead carpenter

    accountability, 34

    as future competition, 146

    defined, 6, 150-151

    mistakes, 20-21, 33

    necessary skills, 21-22, 119-123, 130, 144, 154

    production system, 13

    production time, 143-144, 182

    relationship with contractor, 131-132

    responsibilities, 13-17, 33, 47, 51-60, 154,182

    survey, 181-184

    typical day for, 25-28

Lead carpenter system

    and job-site efficiency, 12-13

    as an evolutionary process, 42, 48-49, 153, 155-156

    as sales tool, 29, 89

    company growth and, 3,7-8, 156-157, 159, 161

    evaluating success of, 48-49

    how it developed, 4

    how it works, 30, 157-158, 160, 162

    implementation plan, 43

    leisure time for contractor and, 8, 30

    longer time to complete jobs, 36, 38, 126

    modifying for small jobs, 9

    modifying for your company, 4, 9

    size of company and, 8

    size of projects and, 8

    source of labor and, 8

    when it's not needed, 8-9

    See also **Growth.**

Leisure time, for contractor, 8, 30

M

Materials

    delivery of, 120-121

    delivery ticket, 27, 121

    ordering and tracking, 120

    takeoffs of, 109-110

    training segment, 199

Meetings

    daily job-site, 128

    for effective communication, 23

    preconstruction, 23, 110-112 115

    See also **Preconstruction meetings.**

Mission statement, training segment, 186

Motivating employees, 122-123. *See also* **Employees.**

N

NARI Lead Carpenter Training Program, 157, 159

Net profit. *See* **Profit.**

Networking, to find lead carpenter, 63

O

Office. *See* **Job-site office.**

One-man crew

    advantages of, 123-126

    safety concerns and, 38-39, 126

    See also **Safety, one-man crews.**

Organizational skills, 21, 45

Overhead

    and profit, 84-85

    costs of lead carpenter offset by efficiency, 32

P

Paperwork

    maintaining on job-site, 17, 28, 34

    system for, 162

Pass-the-baton meeting, 23

People skills, 21-22. *See also* **Lead carpenter, necessary skills; Communication.**

Permits, lead should have, 101

Pickup work, 152

Plans, using current, 97-98, 101

Planning

    for the transition, 41-42

    job-site, 16, 91-118, 94

    See also **Job planning.**

Positive company culture, 37, 145

Preconstruction meetings

    change orders and, 115

    checklist for, 111

    customer relations and, 110, 112

    job-site details, 112

    sales to production crew, 23

    See also **Pass-the-baton meeting.**

Preconstruction tool checklist, 100, 105

Production costs

    components of, 83-85

    how to control, 86-89

    lower with lead carpenter, 32

Production managers
> cost of, 31
> defined, 6
> job description, 77-80
> leads as, 76-77
> production system, 12
> qualifications, 74-76
> when to use, 73-74, 161

Profit
> gross, defined, 88
> importance to lead, 81-82
> increased due to lead carpenters, 31
> net, defined, 88
> net, formula for, 83
> percentages, defined, 88
> problems, sample, 88

Profit sharing. *See* **Employee benefits; Profit sharing.**

Project manager
> commercial projects and, 4
> defined, 6
> supervision of subcontractors, 8

Project schedule, 99. *See also* **Schedule; Scheduling.**

Q

Quality, improved product, 35

R

Remodeling, problems unique to, 4-6

Responsibilities, of lead carpenter, 13-17, 33, 47, 51-60.
> *See also* **Job descriptions.**

S

Safety
> job-site policies, 119
> monitoring, 128-130
> one-man crews and, 38-39, 126
> training segment, 192

Salary. *See* **Compensation.**

Salespeople
> feedback to, 139
> hiring of, 61
> teamwork between leads and, 17-18, 151
> tension between leads and, 151

Schedule
> list format, 114
> Microsoft Project format, 113
> sample form, 99
> weekly, 127

Scheduling
      as lead carpenter's responsibility, 101, 126-127
      as planning tool, 115-117
      of subs, 17
      overruns and effect on costs, 116
      training segment, 198

Site assessment, 94, 97, 102-103. *See also* **Planning, job-site.**

Site superintendent
      defined, 6
      new home development and, 4
      supervision of subcontractors, 8

Special order
      checklist, 96.
      list required by lead, 101, 105

Specifications, checking, 136

Subcontractors
      agreements with lead, 101, 105
      quality control and, 136-137
      scheduling, 138
      supervising, 5-6, 8, 17, 136-138
      training segment, 198

Subtrade, inspection sign-off sheet, 137

T

Takeoffs, of materials, 109-110
Task list, 129
Task management, 126-130
Team, company as, 17-18, 22
Time cards
      training segment, 201
      weekly, 104, 105
Tool checklist, 100, 105
Training
      manual for lead, 70
      of lead, importance, 19-20, 37, 68-69
      on the job, 26, 141
      program, 46, 69-72, 184
      segments, sample training program, 69-71, 185-201
      seminars, 20, 46

W

Wages
      salary vs. wages, 67
      survey of , 183
Warranty calls, 140-141
Weekly time card, 104, 105

Notes

Also Published By The Journal of Light Construction

The Journal of Light Construction is the building industry's leading construction technology magazine. For subscription information, call **(800) 375-5981.**

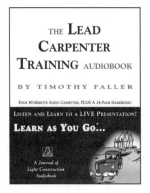

The Lead Carpenter Training Audiobook

The perfect companion to *The Lead Carpenter Handbook*. Based on Tim Faller's popular training workshop, this set of four 90-minute cassette audiotapes is a highly effective training tool, especially for busy contractors and their managers. Includes 24-page reference handbook, including charts, outlines, and forms to help you implement the lead carpenter system.
#TLA99: $49.95

Troubleshooting Guide to Residential Construction

Builders and remodelers have always learned a lot from their mistakes. "Trial and error" is a good — but mighty expensive — teacher. Luckily, it doesn't have to be that way. Now you can reap the benefits of years of on-the-job training without all the hassles, callbacks, and potential liability. You'll find just about every costly construction problem covered in this book, with contributions from over 50 building experts from *The Journal of Light Construction*.
304 pages, 8½ x11, softcover — #TG001: $32.50

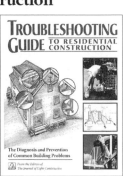

Residential Structure & Framing

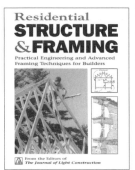

Master the complexities of structural engineering principles and advanced framing techniques with this hands-on guide for builders and remodelers. With simple explanations in plain English, you'll learn how to calculate loads, size joists and beams, and tackle many of the common structural problems faced by residential contractors — including cantilevered floors, complex roof structures, tall window walls, and seismic and wind bracing. Plus, you'll learn field proven production techniques for advanced wall, floor, and roof framing with both dimensional and engineered lumber.

270 pages, 8½ x11, softcover — #SF499: $34.95

The Contractor's Legal Kit

Written in plain English by construction attorney and contractor Gary Ransone, this user-friendly guide gives you a proven approach to running a more profitable business. Includes all the forms, contracts, and practical techniques you need to take control of your jobs from the first client meeting to collecting the last check. All forms and contracts included on IBM-compatible (WINDOWS/DOS) or Mac computer disk.

344 pages, 8½ x11, softcover
Windows/DOS — #LB001: $59.95   **Mac — #LBM01: $64.95**

Managing the Small Construction Business: A Hands-On Guide

An outstanding resource for the builder or remodeler who came up through the trades and is now running his own business — or would like to. With over 70 business articles from *The Journal of Light Construction*, it provides detailed solutions to all the problems and challenges a residential contractor faces.
311 pages, 8½ x11, softcover —
#MS362: $34.95

Advanced Framing: Techniques, Troubleshooting, and Structural Design

How far can I safely cantilever the floor joists? How many collar ties can I remove before the roof sags? You'll find answers to these and hundreds of other questions about residential framing in this best-selling volume from *The Journal*. Over 46 articles with over 250 photos and illustrations.
288 pages, 8½ x11, softcover —
#AF002: $29.95

To order a book or obtain a copy of our full bookstore catalog, please call (800) 859-3669.
Or visit our bookstore online at www.jlcbooks.com.

3\19